THE ENCYCLOPEDIA
OF
PRESIDENT
RONALD REAGAN

THE ENCYCLOPEDIA
OF
PRESIDENT
RONALD REAGAN

Compiled and Edited by:

N.R. Mitgang
&
Malcolm Kushner

ISBN-13: 978-1500768911
ISBN-10: 150076891X

Contact:
NRMitgang@AOL.com
MK@KushnerGroup.com

Photographs Courtesy:
Ronald Reagan Presidential Library

THE HUMOR THAT SHAPED AMERICA
is based on:
Well... There You Go Again!
The Humor That Shaped America

Ronald Reagan | Format: Audio CD
Number of Discs: 2
http://www.amazon.com/There-Again-Humor-Shaped-America/dp/B0030BF6JQ

Dedicated to
Ronald and Nancy Reagan

TABLE OF CONTENTS

MAJOR SPEECHES (VOLUMES TWO AND THREE)

PHOTOGRAPHS (VOLUME FOUR)

* * *

INTRODUCTION

Ronald Reagan's eight-year presidency, one of the most dynamic periods in United States history, resulted in a major refocusing of the nation's social, business and international agenda. No president since F.D.R. has had a greater impact on the American political system.

Domestically, President Reagan presided over the longest peacetime expansion in history, producing a $6 trillion economy. He ended double digit inflation and high interest rates, reduced restrictions on business, implemented tax cuts, and lessened the federal government's responsibility in solving social problems. Internationally, he opposed the Soviet Union and the spread of communism by dramatically increasing defense spending – a policy now credited for achieving America's victory in the Cold War.

This book's creators, N.R. Mitgang & Malcolm Kushner, worked closely with the Ronald Reagan Presidential Library archival and editorial staff to produce this history of an American who loved his country, President Ronald Reagan.

During The Reagan Presidency:

- the 52 American hostages held in Iran for 444 days were released
- Sandra Day O'Connor became the first woman to serve on the Supreme Court
- the Soviets announced the withdrawal of forces from Afghanistan in 1988, ending their futile 8-year war
- Americans received the largest tax cut in United States history
- the United States became the world's largest debtor nation
- the United States and the Soviet Union signed the Intermediate Nuclear Force (INF) Treaty – the first nuclear arms reduction treaty in history
- a new era in United States / Soviet relations began due to the personal relationship between Ronald Reagan and Mikhail Gorbachev
- the Strategic Defense Initiative ("Star Wars") program fundamentally altered United States nuclear defense strategy
- televised congressional hearings of the Iran-Contra affair riveted the nation
- Unemployment hit a 14 year low

Few presidents have enjoyed the affection of so many of the American people. For eight consecutive years President Reagan was, according to the Gallup Polls, the most admired man in America. When Reagan left office in January, 1989, more than 60% of the American people approved of his overall job performance – the highest final approval rating in 40 years.

Much of that popularity was due to his well-honed sense of humor. Known as "The Great Communicator," Reagan was never at a loss for a quip or anecdote to get across a point – a trait that endeared him to political allies and foes alike. His self-effacing stories were legendary. Not since John F. Kennedy has a political leader so captured the hearts and minds of America with humor.

Ronald Reagan is still idolized by millions of Americans who loved him while he was president, and additional millions who have grown to appreciate him since he left the White House.

The bond that Ronald Reagan has forged with the American people is based on his optimism and cemented by his sense of humor. He has always been ready with a quip or anecdote to explain a complex point, lighten a tense moment and bring a smile to America.

Some consider Ronald Reagan's line, "There You Go Again!" as the statement that got him elected President of the United States. Looking at Ronald Reagan through his humor will show how his wit and his ability to touch America's funny bone were his greatest and most powerful political weapons.

* * *

ABOUT THE AUTHORS

The contents of this book are based on the Multimedia Interactive CD-ROM (formerly on display at the Ronald Reagan Presidential Library) and the two-disc comedy album, both entitled:

PRESIDENT RONALD REAGAN
WELL... THERE YOU GO AGAIN!
THE HUMOR THAT SHAPED AMERICA

The Creative Team:

Compiled and Edited by N.R. Mitgang & Malcolm Kushner

N.R. Mitgang

N.R. Mitgang is the former Director of Electronic Publishing and Computer Services for Facts On File Publishers, Inc. (New York). As Director, he created the award-winning CD-ROMs *Facts On File News Digest* and *The American Indian: A Multimedia Encyclopedia. The American Indian* was the first electronic information system available to researchers at the National Archives, Washington, D.C.

Mitgang has more than 40 years of multimedia experience in television, radio, stage, film, books and all forms of electronic publishing. His experience includes work as an acquisitions editor for Grosset & Dunlap, author's agent and author. His writing credits include: co-author, *Mr. Bojangles* (William Morrow Publishers, 1988); co-writer, *I Knew the Man Bojangles* (WNBC-TV, New York, 1989); playwright / lyricist, *Bojangles* (The AMAS Repertory Theatre, New York, 1976); co-author, *The Mirror Lied: One woman's 25-year struggle with bulimia, anorexia, diet pill addiction, laxative abuse and cutting*; author, *Bethann: Love creates a will to survive.* He has also served as a consultant or historical contributor to The Smithsonian Institution, New York City Archives and The National Archives.

Malcolm Kushner

Malcolm Kushner, "America's Favorite Humor Consultant," is an internationally acclaimed expert on humor and communication. Since 1982, he has trained thousands of managers, executives and professionals how to gain a competitive edge with humor. His clients include IBM, Bank of America, Aetna, Infosys, American Bar Association and American Medical Association.

Kushner is the author of *The Light Touch: How to Use Humor for Business Success* (Simon & Schuster), *Public Speaking For Dummies* (Wiley Books) and *Presentations For Dummies* (Wiley Books) which has sold over 100,000 copies.

Frequently interviewed by the media, he has been profiled in *Time Magazine*, *USA Today*, *The New York Times*, *The Washington Post* and numerous other publications. His television and radio appearances include CNN, National Public Radio, CNBC, *Voice of America* and *The Larry King Show*. *The Wall Street Journal* has called him "irrepressible." And his annual "Cost of Laughing Index" appears in print and electronic media around the world.

Kushner holds an M.A. in Communication from the University of Southern California and a J.D. from the University of California Hastings, College of the Law. Prior to becoming a humor consultant, he practiced law with a major San Francisco law firm.

* * *

N.R. Mitgang and Malcolm Kushner would like to thank various members of the Ronald Reagan Presidential Library and National Archives for their help and cooperation in producing this history of an American who loved his country, President Ronald Reagan.

Mitgang and Kushner would also like to thank the current and former members of the Ronald Reagan Presidential Library.

THE REAGAN PRESIDENCY

ECONOMIC POLICY

DOMESTIC AFFAIRS

FOREIGN POLICY

THE REAGAN LEGACY

In his inaugural address after taking the oath of office on January 20, Ronald Reagan called upon Americans to "begin an era of national renewal." In response to the serious problems facing the country, both foreign and domestic, he asserted his familiar campaign phrase: "Government is not the solution to our problem, government is the problem." He hoped that America "will again be the exemplar of freedom and a beacon of hope for those who do not have freedom."

Arguably the first conservative U.S. president in over 60 years, Reagan advanced domestic policies that featured a lessening of federal government responsibility in solving social problems, reducing restrictions on business, and implementing tax cuts. Internationally, Reagan demonstrated a fierce opposition to the spread of communism throughout the world and a strong distrust of the Soviet Union, which in 1983 he labeled an "evil empire." He championed a rearmed and strong military and was especially supportive of the MX missile system and the Strategic Defense Initiative ("Star Wars") program.

ECONOMIC POLICY

When Reagan took office the economy was one of double-digit inflation and high interest rates. During the campaign Reagan promised to restore the free market from excessive government regulation and encourage private initiative and enterprise.

Reagan's economic policies came to be known as "Reaganomics," an attempt, according to Lou Cannon, to "balance the federal budget, increase defense spending, and cut income taxes." The President vowed to protect entitlement programs (such as Medicare and Social Security) while cutting the outlays for social programs by targeting "waste, fraud and abuse." Reagan embraced the theory of "supply side economics," which postulated that tax cuts encouraged economic expansion which in return increased the government's revenue at a lower tax rate.

During his first year in office, Reagan engineered the passage of $39 billion in budget cuts into law, as well as a massive 25 percent tax cut spread over 3 years for individuals, and faster write-offs for capital investment for business. At the same time, he insisted on, and for the most part, was successful in gaining increased funding for defense.

Although inflation dropped from 13.5% in 1980 to 5.1% in 1982, a severe recession set in, with unemployment exceeding 10% in October, 1982 for the first time in forty years. The administration modified its economic policy after two years by proposing selected tax increases and budget cuts to control rising deficits and higher interest rates. After the 1982 downturn, the reduced inflation rate (under 5% for the remainder of the administration) sparked record economic growth, and produced one of the lowest unemployment rates in modern U.S. history (unemployment hit a 14-year low of 5.2% in June 1988). As Reagan left office, the nation was experiencing its sixth consecutive year of economic prosperity.

The economic gains, however, came at a cost of a record annual deficit and a ballooning national debt. The budget deficit was exacerbated by a trade deficit. Americans continued to buy more foreign-made goods than they were selling. Reagan, however, adhered to his free trade stance, and signed an agreement to that effect with Canada. He also signed, reluctantly, trade legislation designed to open foreign markets to U.S. goods.

DOMESTIC AFFAIRS

Reagan's domestic policies had a major impact on the American people and will have for many years. He followed up the passage of the largest tax cut in U.S. history by supporting and signing into law the Tax Reform Act of 1986. Reagan led the battle for a Social Security reform bill designed to insure the long-term solvency of the system, and oversaw the passage of immigration reform legislation, as well as the expansion of the Medicare program to protect the elderly and disabled against "catastrophic" health costs.

Reagan elevated William Rehnquist to the position of Chief Justice of the Supreme Court and appointed three justices to the bench: Anthony Kennedy, Antonin Scalia, and the first woman named to the Supreme Court, Sandra Day O'Connor. In all of the court appointments, Reagan chose individuals who he believed would exercise "judicial restraint."

Reagan consistently received very high approval ratings, although he was not popular with some minority groups, particularly blacks, many of whom failed to benefit from the economic prosperity. In 1986, over 30 percent of the black population had an income level below the official poverty level. While many labor leaders disliked Reagan, especially after he fired the air traffic controllers, when they refused to end their strike (1981), he was popular with union members.

Reagan encouraged the development of "private sector initiatives" as well as federalism, with the objective of transferring from the federal government some of the responsibilities believed to be better served by private business or state and local government.

As the president called for international cooperation to stop the influx of illegal drugs, especially cocaine, into the U.S., First Lady Nancy Reagan, led the campaign against drug abuse, urging the nation's youth to "just say no."

FOREIGN POLICY

At the heart of Reagan's foreign policy was the prevention of communist expansion. This was demonstrated in the Western Hemisphere by the strong financial and military support of the Contras against the Nicaraguan government, the aid given to the government of El Salvador in their fight against the communist guerrillas, and the U.S. invasion of Grenada when that nation was perceived as falling under Cuban domination in 1983, and the support given to rebels fighting Soviet troops in Afghanistan. While efforts for peace in Central America faltered, the Soviets announced the withdrawal of forces from Afghanistan in 1988, ending their futile 8-year war.

Reagan believed that the nation should negotiate with the Soviet Union from a position of strength. To such an end, the administration embarked on a strategic modernization program which included the production of intercontinental ballistic missiles and a feasibility study for the Strategic Defense Initiative. The increase in military spending, and the rise of Mikhail Gorbachev as General Secretary of the Soviet Union at the beginning of Reagan's second term, opened a new era of relations between the two superpowers. After a number of meetings between Reagan and Gorbachev, the two men signed an Intermediate Nuclear Force (INF) Treaty at the Washington Summit in December, 1987. The agreement promised to eliminate an entire class of intermediate-range nuclear missiles and was the first arms control agreement in history to reduce the nuclear arsenal. In addition, the administration began the Strategic Arms Reduction Talks (START) which would reduce the strategic nuclear arsenals by 50%, including large multiple warhead missiles.

When pro-U.S. dictators in Haiti and the Philippines appeared on the verge of being toppled from power, Reagan engineered their safe removal from their countries, insuring bloodless coups and new governments which, he hoped, would be friendly to the U.S.

In Middle East affairs, Reagan reported in his inaugural address that the 52 American hostages held in Iran for 444 days were at that moment being released and would soon return to freedom. The President maintained a firm stance against terrorism, exemplified by the American retaliation against Libya for an air attack in 1981 and again in 1988 for the deaths of Americans in a Berlin Discotheque. Reagan's peacemaking force in war-torn Lebanon experienced tragedy in 1983 when a truck bomb killed 241 soldiers. Tragedy struck again in 1987 when a missile from an Iraqi warplane killed 37 sailors aboard the U.S.S. Stark, part of a U.S. naval taskforce which had been sent to the Persian Gulf to keep that waterway open during the Iran-Iraq war.

The darkest hour of the Reagan administration would become known as the Iran-Contra affair. After lengthy, nationally televised hearings, a special congressional hearings review board reported that Reagan authorized the sale of arms to Iran in exchange for help in freeing U.S. hostages in Lebanon. It was revealed that the money gained from the arms sale was illegally diverted to aid the Contras, opponents of the Nicaraguan Sandinista government. The congressional report criticized Reagan for his detached, hands-off style of management. In the aftermath of the affair, National Security Advisors Robert McFarlane and John Poindexter, as well as National Security Council aide Colonel Oliver North were indicted by a federal grand jury and convicted of lying to Congress.

THE REAGAN LEGACY

The eight years of the Reagan presidency was one of the most dynamic periods, in recent U.S. history, resulting in a major refocusing of the nation's social, business, and international agenda. Few presidents have enjoyed the affection of so many of the American people. Support for Ronald Reagan grew when he was seriously wounded by an assassin's bullet in 1981, and during major surgical procedures in 1985 and 1987. Reagan was known as the "Great Communicator," and often went on television to ask the viewers for their support for a particular piece of legislation. When he ran for a second term in 1984 against former Vice President Walter Mondale, Reagan stood by his record and asked voters if they were better off now than they were 4 years ago. At 73 years of age, Reagan became the oldest man ever elected president, receiving 525 electoral votes, the most of any presidential candidate. As his second term ended, polls showed that more than half of the American people gave him a favorable rating.

When Ronald Reagan became president, he had a clear vision of what the nation should be and spelled out the direction he hoped it would take during his administration. Reagan had a clear social, economic, and foreign policy agenda, and with political guile and personal persuasiveness he was able to achieve many of his goals. Early in his presidency, Reagan remarked: "What I'd really like to do is go down in history as the President who made Americans believe in themselves again."

A month before the election of his successor, Reagan looked back on his eight years in office: "I am the same man I was when I came to Washington," he said, "I believe the same things I believed when I came to Washington, and I think those beliefs have been vindicated by the success of the policies to which we hold fast." About his foreign policy, he said, "At every point on the map that the Soviets have applied pressure, we've done all we can to apply pressure against them." He went on, "And now we are seeing a sight many believed they would never see in our lifetime: the receding of the tide of totalitarianism."

There is little doubt that the many changes effected by the Reagan presidency will play a major role in shaping America's future throughout the 21st century and beyond.

* * *

CHRONOLOGICAL SKETCH OF RONALD REAGAN

February 6, 1911
Ronald Wilson Reagan was born in Tampico, Illinois to Nelle Wilson and John Edward ("Jack") Reagan. The Reagan's had one previous son, Neil ("Moon") Reagan.

1920
The Reagan's moved to a succession of rural northern Illinois towns until they settled in Dixon, Illinois, the place Reagan considered his hometown.

1926
Beginning in 1926, Reagan was employed as a lifeguard at Lowell Park in Dixon. He was credited with saving seventy-seven lives during the seven summers he worked there.

1928
Reagan graduated from Dixon High School. He served as student body president and participated in football, basketball, track, and school plays.

1928-1932
Reagan attended Eureka (Illinois) College, a small liberal arts institution, and majored in economics and sociology. During his sophomore year, Reagan became interested in drama. Reagan also served as student body president.

Franklin Delano Roosevelt's populist rhetoric attracted Reagan to him and later influenced Reagan's speaking style.

1932
Reagan received a temporary sports broadcasting job with WOC, a small radio station in Davenport, Iowa. After WOC consolidated with WHO in Des Moines, "Dutch" recreated Chicago Cubs baseball games from the studio. WHO, an NBC affiliate, gave Reagan national media exposure.

1937
Reagan enlisted in the Army Reserve as a Private but was soon promoted to 2nd Lieutenant in the Officers Reserve Corps of the Cavalry.

An agent for Warner Brothers "discovered" Reagan in Los Angeles and offered him a seven year contract. Reagan played George Gipp in his most acclaimed film, *Knute Rockne – All American* (1940).

January 24, 1940
Reagan and Jane Wyman married. They met while making the movie, *Brother Rat*.

January 4, 1941
Maureen was born.

1942
The Army Air Force called Reagan to active duty and assigned Lt. Reagan to the 1st Motion Picture Unit in Culver City, California, where he made over 400 training films.

July 22, 1943
The Army promoted Reagan to the rank of Captain.

December 9, 1945
The Army honorably discharged Captain Reagan.

1945-1965
Reagan resumed his acting career after the war. Reagan made fifty-three motion pictures and one television movie.

March 18, 1945
Birth of Reagan and Wyman's adopted son, Michael.

1948
Reagan supported Harry S. Truman for president.

1949
Reagan and Wyman divorced.

1950
Reagan campaigned for Helen Gahagan Douglas for the Senate.

1952
Reagan campaigned as a Democrat for Eisenhower.

March 4, 1952
Reagan and Nancy Davis wed.

October 21, 1952
Patricia was born.

Reagan accepted a job as spokesman for the General Electric Company which allowed him to tour the country giving speeches.

1956
Reagan again campaigned as a Democrat for Eisenhower.

May 20, 1958
Ronald Prescott was born.

1960
Reagan campaigned for Richard Nixon for President.

1962
Reagan officially changed his party registration to Republican.

1964
Reagan's television address for Goldwater, "A Time for Choosing," launched his political career. A group of California businessmen soon afterward supported Reagan's candidacy for Governor.

1965
Publication of Reagan's autobiography, "Where's the Rest of Me?"

1966
Reagan defeated incumbent governor Edmund G. ("Pat") Brown. His success in the election and as governor made him a leading contender for the Republican Presidential nomination in 1968.

1968
Reagan made a tentative run for the presidency, waiting until the Republican National convention to announce his candidacy. He later joined in unanimously supporting Richard Nixon.

1970
The voters of California re-elected Reagan Governor.

1974
For several months after leaving the governorship, Reagan wrote a syndicated newspaper column and provided commentaries on radio stations across the country.

November 20, 1975
Reagan announced his candidacy for the Republican nomination for President. Reagan lost the party's nomination but his strong showing laid the groundwork for the election in 1980.

November 13, 1979
Reagan announced his candidacy for President. After winning the party's nomination, he chose George Bush as his running mate. The platform called for "a new consensus with all those across the land who share a community of values embodied in these words: family, work, neighborhood, peace, and freedom."

November 4, 1980
Reagan was elected the 40th President of the United States in a landslide victory over the incumbent, Jimmy Carter.

1981 – THE REAGAN PRESIDENCY

March 30
Assassination attempt by John W. Hinckley, Jr.

July 20-21
Economic Summit, Ottawa.

August 13
Economic Recovery Tax Act.

September 21
Sandra Day O'Connor confirmed as Justice of the Supreme Court.

1982

June 5-6
Economic Summit, Versailles.

1983

May 28-30
Economic Summit, Williamsburg, Virginia.

October 25
U.S. Invasion of Grenada.

1984

June 7-9
Economic Summit, London.

November 4
Reagan re-elected President in landslide victory over Walter Mondale.

1985

May 2-4
Economic Summit, Bonn.

November 19-21
Reagan-Gorbachev Summit, Geneva.

1986

May 4-6
Economic Summit, Tokyo.

September 17
William Rehnquist confirmed as Chief Justice of the Supreme Court; Antonin Scalia confirmed as Justice of the Supreme Court.

October 10-11
Reagan-Gorbachev Summit, Reykjavik

October 22
Tax Reform Act.

November 6
Immigration Reform and control Act.

1987

June 8-10
Economic Summit, Venice

December 8
Reagan and Gorbachev sign the Intermediate Nuclear Force (INF) Treaty at the Summit in Washington, DC.

December 8-10
Reagan-Gorbachev Summit in Washington, DC.

1988

February 3
Anthony Kennedy confirmed as Justice of the Supreme Court.

May 29-June 2
Reagan-Gorbachev Summit in Moscow. The leaders exchanged ratifications of the INF Treaty.

June 19-21
Economic Summit, Toronto.

September 18
U.S.-Canada Free Trade agreement Implementation Act.

November 18
Anti-Drug Abuse Act.

December 7
Final meeting between Reagan and Gorbachev.

2004

June 5, 2004
Ronald Reagan, the 40th President of the United States, died.

* * *

RONALD REAGAN QUOTES

America

In this springtime of hope, some lights seem eternal; America's is.
Remarks Accepting the Presidential Nomination at the Republican National Convention in Dallas, Texas, August 23, 1984

Don't let anyone tell you that America's best days are behind her – that the American spirit has been vanquished. We've seen it triumph too often in our lives to stop believing in it now.
Address Before a Joint Session of the Congress Reporting on the State of the Union, January 26, 1982

America represents something universal in the human spirit. I received a letter not long ago from a man who said, "You can go to Japan to live, but you cannot become Japanese. You can go to France to live and not become a Frenchman. You can go to live in Germany or Turkey, and you won't become a German or a Turk." but then he added, "Anybody from any corner of the world can come to America to live and become an American.
Remarks at a Campaign Rally in San Diego, California, November 7, 1988

But America is too great for small dreams.
Address Before a Joint Session of the Congress on the State of the Union, January 25, 1984

In a world wracked by hatred, economic crisis, and political tension, America remains mankind's best hope.
Remarks at Kansas State University at the Alfred M. Landon Lecture Series on Public Issues, September 9, 1982

All great change in America begins at the dinner table.
Farewell Address to the Nation January 11, 1989

America in the world is only as strong as America at home.
Address Before a Joint Session of Congress on the State of the Union, January 27, 1987

America has always been greatest when we dared to be great. We can reach for greatness again. We can follow our dreams to distant stars, living and working in space for peaceful, economic, and scientific gain. Tonight, I am directing NASA to develop a permanently manned space station and to do it within a decade.
Address Before a Joint Session of Congress on the State of the Union, January 25, 1984

We are a nation that has a government – not the other way around. And that makes us special among the nations of the earth.
Inaugural Address, January 20, 1981

There have been revolutions before and since ours, revolutions that simply exchanged one set of rulers for another. Ours was a philosophical revolution that changed the very concept of government.

> Remarks at the Bicentennial Observance of the Battle of Yorktown in Virginia, October 19, 1981

Our country will always remain the beacon of hope and freedom to all oppressed peoples.

> Radio Address to the Nation on Terrorism, May 31, 1986

Americans

Our country is a special place, because we Americans have always been sustained, through good times and bad, by a noble vision – a vision not only of what the world around us is today but what we as a free people can make it be tomorrow.

> Address Before a Joint Session of the Congress on the State of the Union, January 25, 1983

The task that has fallen to us as Americans is to move the conscience of the world, to keep alive the hope and dream of freedom. For if we fail or falter, there'll be no place for the world's oppressed to flee to.

> Remarks at the Conservative Political Action Conference Dinner February 18, 1983

This country was founded and built by people with great dreams and the courage to take great risks.

> Remarks and a Question-and-Answer Session With Members of the Massachusetts High Technology Council in Bedford, January 26, 1983

Our greatest resources and hope for the future are the minds and hearts of our people.

> Radio Address to the Nation on Administration Policies, August 25, 1984

Well, one of the worst mistakes anybody can make is to bet against Americans.

> Radio Address to the Nation on Free and Fair Trade and the Budget Deficit, May 16, 1987

Bureaucracy

Every once in a while, somebody has to get the bureaucracy by the neck and shake it loose and say Stop what you're doing!

> Remarks and a Question-and-Answer Session With the Students and Faculty at Moscow State University, May 31, 1988

But wouldn't it be better for the human spirit and for the soul of this Nation to encourage people to accept more responsibility to care for one another, rather than leaving those tasks to paid bureaucrats?

Remarks at a White House Luncheon for Black Clergyman, March 26, 1982

Democracy

There's no more striking symbol of democracy than the picture of a citizen casting a ballot, electing a leader, choosing his or her own destiny.

Remarks at a White House Luncheon for Delegates to the Conference on Free Elections, November 4, 1982

The other day, someone told me the difference between a democracy and a people's democracy. It's the same difference between a jacket and a straitjacket.

Remarks on Signing the Human Rights Day, Bill of Rights Day, and Human Rights Week Proclamation, December 10, 1986

In America, our origins matter less than our destination, and that is what democracy is all about.

Republican National Convention, August 17, 1992

Democracy is less a system of government than it is a system to keep government limited, unintrusive: a system of constraints on power to keep politics and government secondary to the important things in life, the true sources of value found only in family and faith.

Remarks and a Question-and-Answer Session With the Students and Faculty at Moscow State University, May 31, 1988

Economy

Saving is one of the best ways people can help themselves and our country. As the pool of savings expands, interest rates come down and billions of dollars are made available for new investments, mortgages, and jobs.

Radio Address to the Nation on the Federal Budget, May 22, 1982

Over the years we've let negative economic forces run out of control. We stalled the judgment day, but we no longer have that luxury. We're out of time.

Address to the Nation on the Economy, February 5, 1981

Government has only two ways of getting money other than raising taxes. It can go into the money market and borrow, competing with its own citizens and driving up interest rates, which it has done, or it can print money, and it's done that. Both methods are inflationary.

    Address to the Nation on the Economy, February 5, 1981

The pounding economic hangover America's suffering from didn't come about overnight. And there's no single instant cure. In recent weeks, a lot of people have been playing what I call the "blame game." The accusing finger has been pointed in every direction of the compass, and a lot of time and hot air have been spent looking for scapegoats. Well, there's plenty of blame to go around.

    Address to the Nation on the Economy, October 13, 1982

The fact is, our deficits come from the uncontrolled growth of the budget for domestic spending.

    Address Before a Joint Session of the Congress on the State of the Union, January 25, 1983

Education

Our leaders must remember that education doesn't begin with some isolated bureaucrat in Washington. It doesn't even begin with state or local officials. Education begins in the home, where it is a parental right and responsibility.

    Remarks to the National Catholic Educational Association in Chicago, Illinois, April 15, 1982

A university is a place where ancient tradition thrives alongside the most revolutionary ideas. Perhaps as no other institution, a university is simultaneously committed to the day before yesterday and the day after tomorrow.

    Address to the Oxford Union Society, Oxford, England, December 4, 1992

Families stand at the center of our society. And every family has a personal stake in promoting excellence in education.

    Address Before a Joint Session of the Congress on the State of the Union, January 25, 1984

Freedom

Freedom is never more than one generation away from extinction. It has to be fought for and defended by each generation.

    Remarks at Annual Convention of Kiwanis International, July 6, 1987

Freedom is not something to be secured in any one moment of time. We must struggle to preserve it every day.

> Remarks on the Anniversary of the Birth of Martin Luther King, Jr., January 15, 1983

In this storm-tossed world of terrorists and totalitarians, America must always champion freedom, for freedom is the one tide that will lead us to the safe and open harbor of peace.

> Radio Address to the Nation on the State of the Union, January 25, 1986

Some people say Americans take our freedom for granted. I think that may be the most glorious gift of all. The Constitution we have makes it possible for all Americans to assume that political freedom is their birthright from the moment they open their eyes.

> Remarks at a Luncheon for Recipients of the Medal of Freedom, November 10, 1988

Above all, we must realize that no arsenal or no weapon in the arsenals of the world is so formidable as the will and moral courage of free men and women.

> Inaugural Address, January 20, 1981

The struggle between freedom and totalitarianism today is not ultimately a test of arms or missiles, but a test of faith and spirit.

> Address Before a Joint Session of the Irish National Parliament, June 4, 1984

We will always remember. We will always be proud. We will always be prepared, so we may always be free.

> Remarks at a United States-France Ceremony Commemorating the 40th Anniversary of the Normandy Invasion, D-day, June 6, 1984

God

If we ever forget that we're one nation under God, then we will be one nation gone under.

> Remarks at the Ecumenical Prayer Breakfast in Dallas, Texas, August 23, 1984

America was founded by people who believed that God was their rock of safety. He is ours. I recognize we must be cautious in claiming that God is on our side, but I think it's all right to keep asking if we're on His side.

> Address Before a Joint Session of the Congress on the State of the Union, January 25, 1984

Our nation's motto − 'In God We Trust' − was not chosen lightly. It reflects a basic recognition that there is a divine authority in the universe to which this nation owes homage.

> Proclamation 4826 − National Day of Prayer, March 19, 1981

The Founding Fathers believed that faith in God was the key to our being a good people and America's becoming a great nation.

Remarks and a Question-and-Answer Session With Women Leaders of Christian Religious Organizations, October 13, 1983

Government

Government is not the solution to our problem; government is the problem.
Inaugural Address, January 20, 1981

Government's first duty is to protect the people, not run their lives.
Address Before a Joint Session of the Tennessee State Legislature, March 15, 1982

We must remove government's smothering hand from where it does harm; we must seek to revitalize the proper functions of government.
Remarks at the Conservative Political Action Conference Dinner, March 20, 1981

Government's first duty is to protect the people, not run their lives.
Remarks at the National Conference of the Building and Construction Trades, AFL-CIO, March 30, 1981

All of us need to be reminded that the Federal Government did not create the States; the States created the Federal Government.
Inaugural Address, January 20, 1981

Respect for human rights is not social work; it is not merely an act of compassion. It is the first obligation of government and the source of its legitimacy.
Address to the 41st Session of the United Nations General Assembly in New York, New York, September 22, 1986

All of us should remember that the federal government is not some mysterious institution comprised of buildings, files and paper. The people are the government. What we create we ought to be able to control.
The President's News Conference, January 29, 1981

We in government should learn to look at our country with the eyes of the entrepreneur, seeing possibilities where others see only problems.
Radio Address to the Nation on Economic Growth, January 26, 1985

Inspirational

We honor the giants of our history not by going back but forward to the dreams their vision foresaw.

Address to the 41st Session of the United Nations General Assembly in New York, New York, February 6, 1985

We have every right to dream heroic dreams. Those who say that we're in a time when there are not heroes, they just don't know where to look.

Inaugural Address, January 20, 1981

There are no such things as limits to growth, because there are no limits on the human capacity for intelligence, imagination and wonder.

Address to the University of South Carolina, Columbia, September 20, 1983

There are no constraints on the human mind, no walls around the human spirit, no barriers to our progress except those we ourselves erect.

Address Before a Joint Session of the Congress on the State of the Union, February 6, 1985

I've always believed that a lot of the trouble in the world would disappear if we were talking to each other instead of about each other.

Remarks at the Ford Claycomo Assembly Plant in Kansas City, Missouri, April 11, 1984

I do not believe in a fate that will fall on us no matter what we do. I do believe in a fate that will fall on us if we do nothing.

Inaugural Address, January 20, 1981

We believed then and now: There are no limits to growth and human progress when men and women are free to follow their dreams.

Inaugural Address, January 21, 1985

Leadership

A leader, once convinced a particular course of action is the right one, must have the determination to stick with it and be undaunted when the going gets rough.

Address to Cambridge Union Society, Cambridge, England, December 5, 1990

The challenge of statesmanship is to have the vision to dream of a better, safer world and the courage, persistence and patience to turn that dream into a reality.

Remarks to the United States Negotiating Team for the Nuclear and Space Arms Negotiations with the Soviet Union, March 8, 1985

Now what should happen when you make a mistake is this: you takes your knocks, you learn your lessons and then you move on. That's the healthiest way to deal with a problem.

Address to the Nation on the Iran Arms and Contra Aid Controversy, March 4, 1987

Military Strength

A truly successful army is one that, because of its strength and ability and dedication, will not be called upon to fight, for no one will dare to provoke it.

Address at Commencement Exercises at the United States Military Academy, May 27, 1981

Military inferiority does not avoid a conflict, it only invites one and then ensures defeat.

Remarks at the Bicentennial Observance of the Battle of Yorktown in Virginia, October 19, 1981

History teaches that wars begin when governments believe the price of aggression is cheap.

Address to the Nation and Other Countries on United States-Soviet Relations, January 16, 1984

The search for peace must go on, but we have a better chance of finding it if we maintain our strength while we're searching.

Address at Commencement Exercises at the United States Military Academy, May 27, 1981

Our military strength is a prerequisite to peace, but let it be clear we maintain this strength in the hope it will never be used, for the ultimate determinant in the struggle that's now going on in the world will not be bombs and rockets, but a test of wills and ideas, a trial of spiritual resolve, the values we hold, the beliefs we cherish, the ideals to which we are dedicated.

Address to Members of the British Parliament, June 8, 1982

Tyrants are tempted by weakness, and peace and freedom can only be preserved by strength.

Radio Address to the Nation on the Observance of Armed Forces Day, May 21, 1983

Americans know an act of Congress can repeal vital military expenditures. They also know what an act of Congress can't repeal: the aggressive tendencies and intentions of our adversaries.

Radio Address to the Nation on Armed Forces Day and Defense Spending, May 18, 1985

Peace

Peace is not the absence of conflict, but the ability to cope with conflict by peaceful means.

Address at Commencement Exercises at Eureka College, Eureka, Illinois, May 9, 1982

A people free to choose will always choose peace.

Remarks and a Question-and-Answer Session With the Students and Faculty at Moscow State University, May 31, 1988

Peace is the highest aspiration of the American People. We will negotiate for it, sacrifice for it, we will never surrender for it, now or ever.
Inaugural Address, January 20, 1981

The search for peace must go on, but we have a better chance of finding it if we maintain our strength while we're searching.
Address at Commencement Exercises at the United States Military Academy, May 27, 1981

Our service men and women know firsthand the horrors of war and the blessings of peace, but they also know that just wanting peace is not enough to guarantee that peace will be sustained.
Radio Address to the Nation on the Observance of Armed Forces Day, May 21, 1983
Enduring peace requires openness, honest communications, and opportunities for our peoples to get to know one another directly. The United States has always stood for openness.
Address to the Nation on the Upcoming Soviet-United States Summit Meeting in Geneva, November 14, 1985

Yet history has shown that peace does not come, nor will our freedom be preserved, by good will alone. There are those in the world who scorn our vision of human dignity and freedom.
Inaugural Address, January 21, 1985

We know that peace follows in freedom's path and conflicts erupt when the will of the people is denied.
Address Before a Joint Session of Congress on the State of the Union, February 4, 1986

We desire peace. But peace is a goal, not a policy. Lasting peace is what we hope for at the end of our journey; it doesn't describe the steps we must take nor the paths we should follow to reach that goal.
Address to the Nation on Strategic Arms Reduction and Nuclear Deterrence, November 22, 1982

When we speak of peace, we should not mean just the absence of war. True peace rests on the pillars of individual freedom, human rights, national self-determination, and respect for the rule of law.
Address to the Nation on the Upcoming Soviet-United States Summit Meeting in Geneva, November 14, 1985

Religion

It's said that prayer can move mountains. Well, it's certainly moved the hearts and minds of Americans in their times of trial and helped them to achieve a society that, for all its imperfections, is still the envy of the world and the last, best hope of mankind.
> Radio Address to the Nation on Prayer, September 18, 1982

The truth is, politics and morality are inseparable. And as morality's foundation is religion, religion and politics are necessarily related. We need religion as a guide. We need it because we are imperfect, and our government needs the church, because only those humble enough to admit they're sinners can bring to democracy the tolerance it requires in order to survive.
> Remarks at an Ecumenical Prayer Breakfast in Dallas, Texas, August 23, 1984

When our Founding Fathers passed the First Amendment, they sought to protect churches from government interference. They never intended to construct a wall of hostility between government and the concept of religious belief itself.
> Remarks at the Annual Convention of the National Association of Evangelicals in Orlando, Florida, March 8, 1983

Social Programs

As I've said before, the only true measure of a welfare program's success is how many people it makes independent of welfare.
> Radio Address to the Nation on Welfare Reform, February 7, 1987

In the past two decades, we have created hundreds of new programs to provide personal assistance. Many of these programs may have come from a good heart, but not all have come from a clear head – and the costs have been staggering.
> Address to the Nation on the Program for Economic Recovery, September 24, 1981

The size of the Federal budget is not an appropriate barometer of social conscience or charitable concern.
> Remarks at the Annual Meeting of the National Alliance of Business, October 5, 1981

Taxes

We don't have a trillion-dollar debt because we haven't taxed enough; we have a trillion-dollar debt because we spend too much.
> Remarks at the National Association of Realtors' Legislative Conference, March 29, 1982

Government does not tax to get the money it needs; government always finds a need for the money it gets.
> Remarks About Federal Tax Reduction Legislation at a White House Luncheon for Out-of-Town Editors and Broadcasters, July 22, 1981

Well, our loyalty lies with little taxpayers, not big spenders. What our critics really believe is that those in Washington know better how to spend your money than you, the people, do. But we're not going to let them do it, period.
> President's News Conference, June 30, 1982

The government is currently experiencing withdrawal symptoms, and we mustn't feed the habit by injecting more tax dollars into it.
> Remarks and a Question-and-Answer Session at a White House Briefing for the Association of Independent Television Stations, January 27, 1982

Only people pay taxes, all the taxes. Government just uses business in a kind of sneaky way to help collect the taxes. They're hidden in the price; we aren't aware of how much tax we actually pay.
> Address to the Nation on the Economy, February 5, 1981

But we cannot reduce the deficit by raising taxes.
> Remarks at the Conservative Political Action Conference, March 1, 1985

Terrorism

Terrorism is the preferred weapon of weak and evil men.
> Remarks at a meeting with members of the American Business Conference, April 15, 1986

When terrorism strikes, civilization itself is under attack; no nation is immune. There's no safety in silence or neutrality. If we permit terrorism to succeed anywhere, it will spread like a cancer, eating away at civilized societies and sowing fear and chaos everywhere.
> Remarks to Citizens in Chicago Heights, Illinois, June 28, 1985

We can never legislate an end to terrorism. However, we must remain resolute in our commitment to confront this criminal behavior in every way – diplomatically, economically, legally, and, when necessary, militarily.
> Statement on Signing the Omnibus Diplomatic Security and Antiterrorism Act of 1986, August 27, 1986

Values

An America that is militarily and economically strong is not enough. The world must see an America that is morally strong with a creed and a vision. We are such people. This is what has led us to dare and achieve. For us, values count.

Remarks at the Annual Convention of the Congressional Medal of Honor Society in New York City, December 12, 1983

Good citizenship and defending democracy means living up to the ideals and values that make this country great.

Remarks to Marine Corps Basic Training Graduates in Parris Island, South Carolina, June 4, 1986

Only our deep moral values and our strong social institutions can hold back that jungle and restrain the darker impulses of human nature.

Remarks at the Annual Meeting of the International Association of Chiefs of Police in New Orleans, Louisiana, September 28, 1981

We've been blessed with the opportunity to stand for something – for liberty and freedom and fairness. And these are things worth fighting for, worth devoting our lives to.

Remarks at the Annual Dinner of the Conservative Political Action Conference, March 1, 1985

Schools that work for the disadvantaged are schools that help their students develop the same qualities of character and the same values that most Americans want for their children. They know there are no such things as black values and white values or poor values and rich values. No, they know there are only basic American values.

Remarks on Receiving the Department of Education Report on Improving Education, May 20, 1987

War

Governments which rest upon the consent of the governed do not wage war on their neighbors.

Address Before a Joint Session of the Congress on the State of the Union, January 25, 1984

There is only one way safely and legitimately to reduce the cost of national security, and that is to reduce the need for it. And this we're trying to do in negotiations with the Soviet Union. We're not just discussing limits on a further increase of nuclear weapons; we seek, instead, to reduce their number. We seek the total elimination one day of nuclear weapons from the face of the Earth.

Inaugural Address, January 21, 1985

There is a profound moral difference between the use of force for liberation and the use of force for conquest.

Remarks at a Ceremony Commemorating the 40th Anniversary of the Normandy Invasion, D-day, June 6, 1984

For it is not people who make war; only governments do that.

Address to the 43d Session of the United Nations General Assembly in New York, New York, September 26, 1988

* * *

THE HUMOR THAT SHAPED AMERICA

Humor may be the best hope for explaining the concepts of a free society.

Every form of humor used by Ronald Reagan during his first and second administrations.

* * *

COMMUNICATION

03/30/81

Building & Construction Trades Department, AFL-CIO: Remarks at the Union's National Conference

There's been a lot of talk in the last several weeks here in Washington about communication and the need to communicate, and the story that I haven't told for a long time – but somehow it's been brought back to me since I've been here – about communication and some of the basic rules of communication.

It was told to me the first time by Danny Villannueva who used to place-kick for the Los Angeles Rams, and then later became a sports announcer, and Danny told me that one night as a sports announcer, he was having a young ballplayer with the Los Angeles Dodgers over to the house for dinner. And the young wife was bustling about getting the dinner ready while he and the ballplayer were talking sports, and the baby started to cry. And over her shoulder, the wife said to her husband, "Change the baby." And this young ballplayer was embarrassed in front of Danny, and he said to his wife, "What do you mean change the baby? I'm a ballplayer. That's not may line of work." And she turned around, put her hands on her hips, and she communicated. She said, "Look buster, you lay the diaper out like a diamond, you put second base on home plate, put the baby's bottom on the pitcher's mound, hook up first and third, slide home underneath, and if it starts to rain, the game ain't called, you start all over again." So I'm going to try to communicate a little bit today.

* * *

BIG GOVERNMENT

02/09/82

Indiana State Legislature: Address Before a Joint Session of the Legislature

In 1919 William Herschell, a columnist for the *Indianapolis News*, came upon another admirer of this State, an old man near Knightstown who was sitting on a log in the warm sunshine, fishing in the Big Blue River. With a sweep of his arm, the old boy encompassed the whole countryside, and he says, "Ain't God good to Indianny!" Well, God certainly has been good to Indiana, but unfortunately over the past few decades, the Federal Government hasn't been quite so kind. If the Federal Government had been around when the Creator was putting His hand to this State, Indiana wouldn't be here. It'd still be waiting for an environmental impact statement.

* * *

01/26/84

Southern Republican Leadership Conference: Remarks to Participants in the Conference in Atlanta, Georgia

I, once as a new Republican, tried to talk the Republican Party into using the 1932 Democratic Platform. It called for a 25-percent reduction in government spending, a return to the States and local communities autonomy that had been confiscated by the Federal Government, a reduction and elimination of useless boards and bureaus and departments in government. And I thought, that's still a brand new platform. At least they've never used it.

* * *

02/09/82
Indiana State Legislature: Address Before a Joint Session of the Legislature

As I pointed out in the State of the Union address, in 1960 the Federal Government had 132 categorical grants costing $7 billion. When I took office there were approximately 500 such grants, costing nearly $100 billion – 13 programs for energy conservation, 36 for pollution control, 66 for social services, 90 for education – and in the Congress it takes at least 166 committees just to try and keep track of them. They try to keep track of them, but Federal grants are like rabbits – they multiply like crazy, and when they're out you can't catch them. The Congress...

The Congress spends most of its time on the budget these programs represent. Governor Babbitt of Arizona said that the Congress should worry about arms control, not potholes. And if Congress did that, he has said, we would have both a better chance of survival and better streets.

I've got to pause right here and interject something about that. I'm delighted in telling about the town that decided in the interest of safety, they were going to raise all their street signs and everything that were only 5 feet high to 7 feet high. And the Federal Government came along and said, "We've got a program that'll do that for you." Well, it was quite an undertaking to change the height of all these. The Federal Government's idea was they'd lower the streets 2 feet.

* * *

08/03/82
Knights of Columbus: Remarks at the Centennial Meeting of the Supreme Council in Hartford, Connecticut

In the last 10 years, Federal spending had tripled. In the last 5 years, Federal taxes had doubled. The philosophy of government seemed to be tax and tax, spend and spend. Now, no one can quarrel with the motive behind all this. It was well-intentioned and done in the name of humanity. The budget for the Department of Health and Human Services became the third largest budget in the world, right after the entire national budgets of the United States and the Soviet Union. The Federal debt reached one trillion dollars, and our interest payments on that debt, in the range of a hundred billion dollars, are more than the entire Federal budget of about 20 years ago.

You know, I have to stop and interject here that, as I said before, this was all done with the best of intentions, all of this was designed to help. But when you set out to help, you'd better have a pretty good idea of what you're doing.

You know, there was a fellow riding a bicycle one cold winter day – a motorcycle, I should say. The wind coming in through the buttons of his leather jacket were chilling him, and finally he stopped, turned the jacket around, put it on backwards, took off again. Well, that solved the wind problem, but he hit a patch of ice; his arms were kind of restricted; he skidded into a tree. And when the police got there and elbowed their way through the crowd that had gathered and they said, "What happened?" They said, "We don't know. When we got there, he seemed to be all right. But by the time we had his head turned around straight, he was dead."

* * *

03/01/82

The State of Small Business: Remarks at a White House Briefing for Small Business Leaders

I just have to interject here a little incident that happened to me in the first real ranch that I ever – after dreaming of it – owned. So, I had 50 head of steers, grazer cattle there. And one day I got a notification from the State that I was to get them all in a corral, because the State veterinarians were going to come in and check them. I was in a brucellosis area.

Well now, brucellosis is a disease that affects cows' milk, none of which steers have. And so, at great effort and sweat we got them in the corral. And then they came, and every one of them had to be run into a squeeze chute for the examination and the shot. And I was kind of curious about this – and I said to the doctor, I said, "Well, tell me, if you found brucellosis here in any of them, what happens?" "Oh, well, then," he says, "you have to sell them." And I said, "I have to sell them?" He said "Yes." He said, "It doesn't affect the beef. So," he said, "you'd sell them." And then he said, "You'd get $75 in State and Federal bonus for having to sell them."

And I said, "Wait a minute, let me get this straight." I said, "I sell them, and I get to keep the money I sell them for, plus $75 a head for every one that I sell?" And he said, "Yes." And I said, "I only have one more question. Where can I find a lot of cattle with brucellosis?"

* * *

05/10/82

YMCA of Metropolitan Chicago: Remarks at the Annual Foundation Luncheon

Over the last decade Federal spending tripled at the same time that defense spending decreased in constant dollars. Federal social spending increased over the last three decades eight times more than prices.

Some of the programs established during that spending binge remind me of the preacher who had come to a small hamlet about a hundred miles from his own home-town to preach at a revival meeting. And driving into the village he noticed a man from his own community, a fellow that was rather known for his drinking, who was sitting on the front steps of the general store. And he stopped his car and he asked the drinker why he was so far from home and was told that beer was 5 cents a bottle cheaper there. Well, when the minister pointed out the cost of travel back and forth, the price for a hotel room, the beer drinker retorted, "I'm not stupid, Reverend. I just sit here and drink till I show a profit."

* * *

12/10/84

President's Citation Program for Private Sector Initiatives: Remarks at a Ceremony Marking the Beginning of the Awards Program

The American people saw what was happening, and when George Bush and I were elected they gave us a mandate which we interpreted as "end the waste and, wherever possible, shift the focus away from the slow-moving labors of the bureaucrats back to the caring and efficient efforts of the people themselves."

I treasure one story, an experience that happened before I came here. There was a gentleman whose social security payments stopped coming. And when he inquired, they said he was dead. He said he wasn't. Finally... You know, when a computer makes a mistake, it's a mistake. Finally he went in person and informed them that there he was, in the living flesh. And the computer said he was dead, and there wasn't anything that they could do.

He'd been without the payments; he was destitute. And they – at least, thank heaven, there was someone there that turned to voluntarism in a way – they temporarily solved his problem while they went to work to try and solve it permanently. They gave him the social security funeral allowance to tide him over.

* * *

CHANGING GOVERNMENT TAKES TIME

02/26/82

Conservative Political Action Conference: Remarks at the Conference Dinner

And I hope you realize it's going to take more than 402 days to completely change what's been going on for 40 years.

I realized that the other day when I read a story about a private citizen in Louisiana who asked the government for help in developing his property. And he got back a letter that said, "We have observed that you have not traced the title prior to 1803. Before final approval, it will be necessary that the title be traced previous to that year." Well, the citizen's answer was eloquent.

"Gentlemen," he wrote, "I am unaware that any educated man failed to know that Louisiana was purchased from France in 1803. The title of the land was acquired by France by right of conquest from Spain. The land came into the possession of Spain in [1842] 1492 by right of discovery by an Italian sailor, Christopher Columbus. The good Queen Isabella took the precaution of receiving the blessing of the Pope... The Pope is emissary of the Son of God, who made the world. Therefore, I believe that it is safe to assume that He also made that part of the United States called Louisiana. And I hope to hell you're satisfied."

* * *

06/20/83

Mississippi Republican Party Fundraising Dinner: Remarks at the Dinner Honoring Representative Trent Lott in Jackson, Mississippi

We have canceled 73 million copies of Federal publications. We have eliminated 2,200 various publications, bulletins, and reports and so forth, such as "How to Buy a Christmas Tree." And then there was a regular one they put out – and I just happened to take that one off the Cabinet table today and bring it along, because I thought it was pretty indicative of the kind of thing that government's been doing. It's "How to Have a Sparkling Clean Sink" – kitchen sink.

Now, the very top of it illustrates why they had to keep this bulletin out for you people. It said, "A clean sink helps keep you and your family healthy. A dirty sink often smells bad. It will attract bugs. For a clean kitchen you need a clean sink." And the last point is, "A clean sink looks nice." Now, you ladies know you'd never have thought of that by yourselves if the government hadn't pointed it out to you.

* * *

09/28/81

Louisiana Republican Reception: Remarks at the Fundraising Reception

I've just spoken to a national meeting here in your city a few moments ago, the police chiefs of not only the Nation but internationally – sheriffs – tremendous crowd. I spoke to them about crime, and I'm happy to tell you that they're against it.

But you know talking about some of the problems in Washington right now is a little like an Irish landlady who put up a lunch every day for one of her boarders that he took to work. And he was always unhappy about the lunch and let her know when he came home. So, she put two slices of bread in, and the next day she put in four, and he was still unhappy. And then she put in six, and he was unhappy. She got up to about 10, and he was still griping about the quality of the lunch, so she split a loaf of bread, put ham between the two halves, and put that in the lunch. He came home, and she was waiting for him and said, "How was the lunch?" He said, "Well, all right. But I see you're back to two slices again."

***

03/20/81
Conservative Political Action Conference: Remarks at the Conference

Now, obviously, we're not going to be able to accomplish all this at once. The American people are patient. I think they realize that the wrongs done over several decades cannot be corrected instantly.

You know I had the pleasure in appearing before a Senate Committee once while I was still Governor and I was challenged because there was a Republican President in the White House, who had been there for several months, why we hadn't then corrected everything that had been done. And the only way I could think to answer him was... I told him about a ranch many years ago that Nancy and I acquired, had a barn with 8 stalls in it in which they had kept cattle and we wanted to keep horses and I was in there day after day with a pick and a shovel lowering the level of those stalls which had accumulated over the years.

And I told this Senator, who had asked that question, that I discovered that you did not undo in weeks or months what had taken some fifteen years to accumulate.

I also believe that we conservatives, if we mean to continue governing, must realize that it will not always be so easy to place the blame on the past for our national difficulties. You know, one day the great baseball manager Frankie Frisch sent a rookie out to play center field. The rookie promptly dropped the first fly ball that was hit to him. On the next play he let a grounder go between his feet and then threw the ball to the wrong base. Frankie stormed out of the dugout, took his glove away from him and said, "I'll show you how to play this position." And the next batter slammed a line drive right over second base. Frankie came in on it, missed it completely, fell down when he tried to chase it, threw down his glove and yelled at the rookie, "You've got centerfield so screwed up nobody can play it."

***

RELIGION – Part One

08/31/84
Catholic Golden Age Association: Remarks to Chapter Presidents of the Association

Now, there are a number of things I want to talk about today, and I'm going to get to it. But since we'll be talking about Federal programs that have had some problems, I want to tell you a story that I heard about how such problems can happen anywhere.

Please don't think me irreligious, but the story goes that one day Saint Peter was happily walking around near the Pearly Gates, and he heard a funny little sound and saw a lot of little things scurrying about and realized that heaven had a new delegation of mice. And he leaned down and talked to them, and he said, "How do you like it up here?" And they said, "Well, the accommodations are superb." But they had a complaint. They said heaven is so large, their legs were so short, that it was hard for them to get around and see everything. So, Saint Peter ordered that they all be given roller skates. And they put them on, and the next day they were darting all over, having a heck of a time there. And a week later, St. Peter went for his stroll – and no mice. He looked around, and he couldn't find them. And all of sudden he came upon a fat and happy old cat that was sleeping in the corner. And he said, "Well, cat, how are you doing? How do you like heaven?" And the cat said, "It's paradise. It's clean it's quite, the weather's nice, and those meals on wheels – delicious."

* * *

02/03/83
National Prayer Breakfast: Remarks at the Annual Breakfast

You know, on the way over, I remembered something that happened a long time ago when teachers could talk about things like religion in the classroom. And a very lovely teacher was talking to her class of young boys, and she asked, "How many of you would like to go to heaven?" And all the hands instantly shot into the air at once, except one, and she was astounded. And she said, "Charlie, you mean you don't want to go to heaven?" He said, "Sure, I want to go to heaven, but not with that bunch."

Maybe there's a little bit of Charlie in each of us.

* * *

03/08/83
National Association of Evangelicals: Remarks at the Annual Convention in Orlando, Florida

From the joy and the good feeling of this conference, I go to a political reception. Now, I don't know why, but that bit of scheduling reminds me of a story – which I'll share with you.

An evangelical minister and a politician arrived at Heaven's gate one day together. And St. Peter, after doing all the necessary formalities, took them in hand to show them where their quarters would be. And he took them to a small, single room with a bed, a chair, and a table and said this was for the clergyman. And the politician was a little worried about what might be in store for him. And he couldn't believe it when St. Peter stopped in front of a beautiful mansion with lovely grounds, many servants, and told him that these would be his quarters.

And he couldn't help but ask, he said, "But wait, how – there's something wrong – how do I get this mansion while that good and holy man only gets a single room?" And St. Peter said, "You have to understand how things are up here. We've got thousands and thousands of clergy. You're the first politician who ever made it."

* * *

11/16/82
U.S. League of Savings Associations: Remarks at the League's 90th Annual Convention in New Orleans, Louisiana

You know, thinking about what your group has been through reminds me of the story of the three gentlemen who had departed this Earth and were standing at the gates of heaven waiting for admittance. One was a surgeon, the other one an engineer, the third one an economist. They'd all been good, upright people, but it developed that there was only room inside for one. So St. Peter said, "I'll tell you what, I'll pick the one who comes from the oldest profession." The surgeon stepped right up and he said, "Well, I'm your man. Right after God created Adam, he operated. He took a rib, created Eve, so surgery has to be the oldest profession." And the engineer said, "Whoops. No." He said, "You see, before God created Adam and Eve, he took the chaos that prevailed and built Earth in 6 days. So engineering had to precede surgery." The economist spoke up and said, "Just a minute. Who do you think created all that chaos?"

* * *

01/26/84
Southern Republican Leadership Conference: Remarks to Participants in the Conference in Atlanta, Georgia

Thank you. I'll take that under consideration until Sunday night. Well, I thank you Mack [Mattingly] and Bill Harris, Bob Bell, and Members of the Congress, Newt Gingrich, and ladies and gentlemen.

I have to tell you a little something here that's just reminded me of a story – two things have reminded me. First of all, I understand that many of you heard me last night, and then I happened to hear that a great many of you heard me on television just a little while ago. And the other thing is when two gentlemen came in here, that left me backstage with their wives. And that also helped remind me of the story. It happens to be a story of an older preacher who was talking to a young preacher who hadn't had as much experience.

And he said to him, "You know, sometimes on Sunday morning, they begin to nod off." And he says, "I've found a way to wake them up." He says, "Right in my sermon when I see them beginning to doze, I say, `Last night I held in my arms a woman who is the wife of another man.'" And he says, "That wakes them up." And he says, "Then, when they look at me startled, I say: It was my dear mother."

Well, the young preacher took that to heart. And a few weeks later, sure enough, there some of them were dozing off. So, he remembered what had been told him, and he said, "Last night I held in my arms a woman who is the wife of another man." And they all looked at him, and everyone was awake. And he says, "I can't remember who it was."

* * *

07/27/82
Future Farmers of America: Remarks to Representatives of the Youth Organization

I don't know whether you know the story about the old boy that had taken over some land down in a creek bottom – and it was covered with rocks and brush, and it was pretty scrabbly – and he went to work on it.

And he worked and worked, and finally he had a garden that was his pride and joy. And one Sunday morning after the Sunday services he asked the minister if he wouldn't like to come out and see his garden. Well, the minister arrived and he looked. And he looked at melons, and he said, "Oh, the Lord has certainly blessed this land." And he looked at some corn – he said the tallest he'd ever seen. He said, "The Lord has blessed this land." He said, "My, what the Lord and you have managed to accomplish here." And he went on that way for about 10 minutes. And the old boy finally said, "Reverend, I wish you could have seen this when the Lord was doing it by himself."

* * *

09/26/83
Challenge Grant Amendments of 1983: Remarks on Signing S. 1872 into Law

And I can't help but tell a little story I heard the other day about faith. A fellow fell off a cliff, and as he was falling grabbed a limb sticking out the side of the cliff and looked down 300 feet to the canyon floor below and then looked up and said, "Lord, if there's anyone up there, give me faith. Tell me what to do." And a voice from the heavens said, "If you have faith, let go." He looked down at the canyon floor and then took another look up and said, "Is there anyone else up there?"

* * *

03/16/81
Associated General Contractors of America: Remarks at a Reception

We can bring inflation down, and we can get America building again. You know, if that sounds like we're asking for miracles, well, on this eve of St. Patrick's Day, someone with the name of Reagan I think is entitled to think in terms of miracles.

You know, there was a little tad that was in court in New York, bandaged from his toes to his chin, suing for $4 million as the result of an accident, and he won the suit. The lawyers for the insurance company went over to him, and they said, "You're never going to enjoy a penny of this. We're going to follow you 24 hours a day. We know you're faking, and the first time you move, we'll have you." He said, "Will you now? Well," he said, "Let me tell you what's going to happen to me." He said, "They're coming in here with a stretcher. They're taking me out, and downstairs they're putting me in a car – in an ambulance. They're driving me straight to Kennedy Airport, and they're putting me on the airplane on that stretcher. We're flying direct to Paris, France, and there they're taking me on the stretcher off the plan, putting me in another ambulance. We're going direct to the Shrine of Lourdes, and there you're going to see the damnedest miracle you ever saw."

* * *

COMMUNISM

06/22/83
National Federation of Independent Business: Remarks at the National Conference of the Federation

The principles of wealth creation transcend time, people, and place. Governments which deliberately subvert them by denouncing God, smothering faith, destroying freedom, and confiscating wealth have impoverished their people. Communism works only in heaven, where they don't need it, and in hell, where they've already got it.

* * *

05/09/82
Eureka College: Remarks at the Alumni Association Dinner in Peoria, Illinois

But to those who were there today, I told them of a little story that illustrates the humor of the Russian people and their cynicism about their way of life and their government. And I had to choose between two. So, I won't repeat the one that I told there today – but the one I wanted to tell and didn't – and this is truly – the jokes – I've come to be a collector of these that the Russian people tell among themselves that reveals their feeling about their government.

And it has to do with when Brezhnev first became President. And he invited his elderly mother to come up and see his suite of offices in the Kremlin and then put her in his limousine and drove her to his fabulous apartment there in Moscow. And in both places, not a word. She looked; she said nothing. Then he put her in his helicopter and took her out to the country home outside Moscow in a forest. And, again, not a word. Finally, he put her in his private jet and down to the shores of the Black Sea to see that marble palace which is known as his beach home. And finally she spoke. She said, "Leonid, what if the Communists find out?"

* * *

08/12/83

U.S. Hispanic Chamber of Commerce: Remarks at the Fourth Annual Convention in Tampa, Florida

You know, I have to interrupt and tell you something, 'cause I just heard a little joke that I think some people in Cuba are telling. Castro was making a speech to a large audience, and he said, "They say that I am – accuse me of intervening in Angola." And a man going through the audience said, "Peanuts, popcorn." He said, "They say that I'm intervening in Mozambique," and the same voice said, "Peanuts and popcorn." And he said, 'They say that I'm intervening in Nicaragua." "Peanuts and popcorn." And by this time he's boiling mad, and he said, "Bring that man who's shouting 'peanuts and popcorn' to me, and I'm going to kick him all the way to Miami." And everybody in the audience started shouting, "Peanuts and popcorn."

* * *

WASHINGTON

09/12/84

Dinner Honoring Senator Howard H. Baker, Jr.: Remarks at the "Roast" for the Senate Majority Leader

And he told me on the steps of the Capitol, at the time of the Inaugural 4 years ago, he said, "Mr. President, I want you to know I will be with you through thick." And I said, "What about thin?" He said, "Welcome to Washington."

* * *

02/26/82

Conservative Political Action Conference: Remarks at the Conference Dinner

But Washington's fascination with passing trends and one-day headlines can sometimes cause serious problems over in the West Wing of the White House – they cause them. There's the problem of leaks. Before we even announced the give-away of surplus cheese, the warehouse mice had hired a lobbyist.

And then a few weeks ago, those stories broke about the Kennedy tapes. And that caused something of a stir. Al Haig came in to brief me on his trip to Europe. I uncapped my pen, and he stopped talking. And, up on the Hill, I understand they were saying, "You need eloquence in the State Dining Room, wit in the East Room, and sign language in the Oval Office." It got so bad that I found myself telling every visitor there were absolutely no tape recordings being made. And if they wanted a transcript of that remark, just mention it to the potted plant on their way out.

* * *

02/21/83

National Review: Remarks at Reception Honoring the Magazine

You know, I've often thought when I've been faced with memorandums from deep in the bowels of the bureaucracy what I wouldn't give to have Bill as an interpreter.

You know, a fellow comes in, stands in front of your desk, hands you a memorandum, and he stays and waits there while you read it. And so you read: "Action-oriented orchestration, innovation, inputs generated by escalation of meaningful, indigenous decisionmaking dialog, focusing on multilinked problem complexes, can maximize the vital thrust toward nonalienated and viable urban infrastructure." I take a chance and say, "Let's try busing." And if he walks away, I know I guessed right.

* * *

02/18/83

Conservative Political Action Conference: Remarks at the 10th Annual Conference Dinner

Now, I know there's concern over attempts to roll back some of the gains that we've made. And it seems to me that here we ought to give some thought to strategy – to making sure that we stop and think before we act. For example, some of our critics have been saying recently that they want to take back the people's third-year tax cut and abolish tax indexing. And some others, including members of my staff, wanted immediately to open up a verbal barrage against them. Well, I hope you know that sometimes it's better if a President doesn't say exactly what's on his mind. There's an old story about a farmer and a lawyer that illustrates my point.

It seems that these two got into a pretty bad collision, a traffic accident. They both got out of their cars. The farmer took one look at the lawyer, walked back to his car, got a package, brought it back. There was a bottle inside, and he said, "Here, you look pretty shook up. I think you ought to take a nip of this, it'll steady your nerves." Well, the lawyer did. And the farmer said, "You still look a little bit pale. How about another?" And the lawyer took another swallow. And under the urging of the farmer, he took another and another and another. And then, finally, he said he was feeling pretty good and asked the farmer if he didn't think that he ought to have a little nip too. And the farmer said, "Not me, I'm waiting for the State trooper."

* * *

DEMOCRATS

08/11/82

Billings, Montana: Remarks at a Fundraising Luncheon for the Republican Candidate for U.S. Senator from Montana

As I've said before, no matter how tough my job gets, sometimes I wake up at night in a cold sweat thinking how much worse it could be if we didn't have a Republican majority in the Senate. As I said to a little group just a short time ago, imagine having two Tip O'Neills.

* * *

06/20/83

Mississippi Republican Party Fundraising Dinner: Remarks at the Dinner Honoring Representative Trent Lott in Jackson, Mississippi

But isn't it wonderful to see so many Republicans in Mississippi? Times have changed and for the better. Former Congressman Prentiss Walker, who I understand is here today, tells a story about his first campaign. He dropped in on a farm and introduced himself as a Republican candidate. And as he tells it, the farmer's eyes lit up, and then he said, "Wait till I get my wife. We've never seen a Republican before."

And a few minutes later he was back with his wife, and they asked Prentiss if he wouldn't give them a speech. Well, he looked around for a kind of a podium, something to stand on, and then the only thing available was a pile of that stuff that the late Mrs. Truman said it had taken her 35 years to get Harry to call "fertilizer." So, he stepped up on that and made his speech. And apparently he won them over. And they told him it was the first time they'd ever heard a Republican. And he says, "That's okay. That's the first time I've ever given a speech from a Democratic platform."

* * *

08/24/84

Dallas, Texas: Remarks to Members of the Republican National Committee and the Reagan-Bush Campaign Staff

Things are going so well that the opposition has had to reverse the meaning of a few words and concepts. Indeed, at their meeting in San Francisco, one of their speakers called the economic expansion – and I quote – an "illusion." Well, it's pretty hard to cash an illusion. People are cashing bigger checks.

But according to the opposition, prosperity is an illusion. Strong defenses – and this again is quoting them – are "destabilizing." And if you read the record of the last administration backward, it has a happy ending.

* * *

10/15/84

Tuscaloosa, Alabama: Remarks at a Question and Answer Session with Students at the University of Alabama-Tuscaloosa

I think my opponent's economic policies and programs are about as bad as they can be. And when he comes down here and says his ideas are best for the South, he's handing you the ultimate Mason-Dixon Line. You know, buying his economic policies is like going to a used-car lot to buy back the lemon you sold them 4 years ago.

* * *

02/07/84

Nevada Republican Party Fundraising Luncheon: Remarks at the Luncheon in Las Vegas, Nevada

Life not only begins at 40, but so does lumbago and the tendency to tell the same story over and over again. So, if you've heard it, just be polite and pretend you haven't.

It's about a little boy who was selling some puppies that he had to get rid of. And he set up shop right outside a Democratic fundraiser. And when the people began coming out, and one couple stopped and looked, and then, joshingly, the man said, "Are those Democrat puppies?" And he said, "Oh, yes, sir." Well, the couple wound up buying one.

Well, the next week the Republicans were having a fundraiser, and he set up shop again – same location and some of the same pups. And out came the people and, sure enough, somebody asked him if they were Republican pups. And he said, "Yes." And he sold one. And a newspaper reporter who was nearby and had been present the week before said, "Hey, kid, wait a minute. Last week you said those were Democrat pups. Now you're saying they're Republicans." And the kid says. "Yeah." And he says, "Well, how come?" He says, "That's easy." He says, "This week they got their eyes open."

* * *

THE PRESIDENT'S AGE

01/26/82
State of the Union Address (Social Programs Transferred to States): Joint Session of Congress

Today marks my first State of the Union Address to you, a Constitutional duty as old as our Republic itself. President Washington began this tradition in 1790 after reminding the Nation that the destiny of self-government and the "preservation of the sacred fire of liberty" is "finally staked on the experiment entrusted to the hands of the American people." For our friends in the press, who place a high premium on accuracy, let me say, I did not actually hear George Washington say that.

* * *

02/04/82
National Prayer Breakfast: Remarks at the Annual Breakfast

Last year you all helped me begin celebrating the 31st anniversary of my 39th birthday. And I must say that all of those pile up, an increase of numbers, don't bother me at all, because I recall that Moses was 80 when God commissioned him for public service, and he lived to be 120. And Abraham was 100 and his wife Sarah 90 when they did something truly amazing – and he lived to be 175. Just imagine if he had put $2,000 a year into his IRA account.

* * *

02/09/82
National Religious Broadcasters: Remarks at the Organization's 39th Convention

America's elderly are a wise and a very precious resource, and we should always honor them and never set them aside. I know that people in that generation – in "our" generation – are sometimes a bit sensitive about their age. I was kidded myself again last week, as I celebrated the 32nd anniversary of my 39th birthday. But then I remembered something that Thomas Jefferson said. He said that we should never judge a President by his age; we should judge him by his work. And ever since he told me that, I've stopped – I've stopped worrying. I have increased the workload a little.

* * *

02/06/84

Eureka, Illinois: Remarks to Students and Faculty at Eureka College

I want you to know that this has been a day that – if I said, Neil, you wouldn't know who I was talking about – my brother, Moon, and I will long remember. It's a day of warmth and memory, a day when the good things that have happened in our lives all seem very close and very real again.

We've just come from Dixon, where I attended my biggest birthday party ever. It was the 34th anniversary of my 39th birthday. And I had what every man who has that many candles on his birthday cake needs around him – a large group of friends and a working sprinkler system.

And now we're here for Eureka's birthday. Legend has it that after Ben Major led a wagon train here, he sunk an ax into the first tree he felled and said, "Here we'll build our school." And that was, as you've been told, more than 129 years ago. And just to end any speculation going on among the undergraduates, no, I was not a part of that original wagon train.

It's always wonderful to return to Eureka. People ask me if I'm looking back at my college years, if I can remember any inkling that I would someday run for President. Well actually, the thought first struck me on graduation day, when the president of the college handed me my diploma and asked, "Are you better off today than you were 4 years ago?"

* * *

EDUCATION

06/22/81

Champions of American Sport: Remarks at a White House Reception

It was sports heroes in my day that created in me the ambition to participate in sports – first in high school and then in college. Indeed, if it hadn't been for football, track, and swimming, I might not have been able to go to college. We didn't have athletic scholarships in those days. We had to do things like wind the clock in the gym. But I loved it when it was plain and simple and honorable.

* * *

07/29/83

National Association of Elementary School Principals and National Association of Secondary School Principals: Remarks at a White House Reception for Association Members

Well, thank you all. And let me welcome you all to the White House. You know, I've been out of school for a little over 50 years now, but I still get nervous around so many principals. And I don't know why I should think of this story except that it has to do with school, and I know that – and teachers, and I know also that it's very dangerous to ever try to tell stories to people of one profession about their profession. But I'll take a chance anyway.

It was the teacher that was trying to impress on her students, the children – winter had come along and the cold season and all. And she was trying to tell them how to – the need to avoid catching colds. And so, she told a very heart-rending tale which she said was about her one-time little brother. And she said that – told her little brother that – or the class that she had this little brother and that he has a fun-loving little boy, and he went out with his sled. And he stayed out too long, and he caught cold. And that was pneumonia, and three days later he was dead. And when she'd finished with the tale, the way she told it, there was just dead silence in the room. And she thought she really gotten to them. And then a voice in the back said, "Where's his sled?"

* * *

08/03/82

Knights of Columbus: Remarks at the Centennial Meeting of the Supreme Council in Hartford, Connecticut

We believe that school children deserve the same protection, the same constitutional consensus that permits prayer in the Houses of Congress, chaplains in our armed services, and the motto on our coinage that says, "In God We Trust." I grant you, possibly we can make a case that prayer is needed more in Congress than in our schools, but – *** * ***

THE IRISH

02/18/83

Conservative Political Action Conference: Remarks at the 10th Annual Conference Dinner

I'm grateful to the American Conservative Union, Young Americans for Freedom, National Review, and Human Events for organizing this third annual memorial service for the Democratic platform of 1980. Someone asked me why I wanted to make it three in a row. Well, you know how the Irish love wakes.

* * *

03/17/81

St. Patrick's Day: Toast at a Luncheon Hosted by the Irish Ambassador

I'm honored to have received your traditional shamrocks, which symbolize this day and the friendship between our two countries, and I'm especially pleased and most grateful for the beautiful scroll of the Reagan family tree. Up on the Hill this morning at a meeting with some of the legislative leadership – Mr. Speaker, on our side of the aisle – Senator Laxalt presented me with a great green button that he thought I should wear, which said "Honorary Irishman." And I said so that son of the Basques – "I'm not honorary; I am."

* * *

03/16/84

Visit of Prime Minister Garret FitzGerald of Ireland: Toasts at the Luncheon

I have to pause for a second. I've already told this to some of you, but I have to tell the rest because I know that Father Hesburgh is here in the room someplace from Notre Dame. Back in the days of the great Knute Rockne when Notre Dame was the giant of the football world, it was between halves one day at a game, when the officials came into the locker room and said to Rockne that the other team was complaining that the Notre Dame players in the pile-ups were biting them. And he said, "We can't fine them, of course, and, Rock, what do you think we should do?" And Rock says, "Tell them next year to play us on Friday."

But so many of our great public figures are of Irish ancestry, from the man considered by many as the father of the American Navy, John Barry, to our first heavyweight champion, John L.

Sullivan, to the great tenor, John McCormack, to a couple of Presidents of the United States and, yes, even to the current Speaker of the House.

In fact, the secret wish disclosed the other day by my friend, Tip O'Neill, is an indication of the hold that Ireland has on all of us here in the States. This is a nation where the Speaker of the U.S. House of Representatives aspires to someday be Ambassador to Ireland. Tip, what about day after tomorrow?

* * *

06/23/82
Intelligence Identities Protection Act of 1982: Remarks on Signing H.R. 4 Into Law

Thank you very much. You know, I tried to bring a former Director of your organization over here with me this morning, Vice President George Bush, but unfortunately, they had him scheduled elsewhere. But I told him I would give him personal credit, because I'm going to tell you a story that I think may be is kind of appropriate for this occasion.

It's one of the few stories that I can tell anymore because it's Irish and my name is Reagan so, therefore, I'm not telling an ethnic joke when I tell this story. But the story has to do – and I know this is dangerous, because anytime you go to a meeting and some people – a trade joke about their trade – they may have heard it before you did. But anyway, I'll try.

It has to do with a gentleman who was stationed in a little town on an errand in Ireland and the agency had to get to him in an emergency situation and called in someone else and said, "Now, you'll go there. You'll contact him. His name is Murphy, and the recognition will be, you'll say, `Well, `tis a fair day, but it'll be lovelier this evening.'"

So, he goes to the little town, goes into the pub, elbows up to the bar and orders a drink, and then just casually says to the bartender, "Say, how would I get in touch with Murphy?" And the bartender says, "Well, if it's Murphy the farmer you want, he's 2 miles down the road, and the farm on the left. If it's Murphy the shoemaker you want, he's on the second floor of the building across the street. And, my name is Murphy." So, he picked up his drink, and he said, "Well, 'tis a fair day, but it'll be lovelier this evening." He says "Oh, it's Murphy the spy you want. Well..."

* * *

11/06/81
American Irish Historical Society: Remarks at the Society's 84th Annual Dinner

And we walked with great interest and looked at those ancient tombstones and the inscriptions.

And then we came to one and the inscription said: "Remember me as you pass by, for as you are, so once was I. But as I am, you too will be, so be content to follow me." And that was too much for the Irish wit and humor of someone who came after, because underneath was scratched: "To follow you I am content, I wish I knew which way you went."

* * *

FISHING AND FARMING

03/17/81
National Association of State Departments of Agriculture: Remarks at a Dinner Honoring Secretary of Agriculture John R. Block

You know, I have to tell you that this has been quite a day. I had lunch at the Irish embassy. It happened to be an appropriate occasion for that today. And before I left, it's the most infectious brogue in the world, before I left, I was talking like, "Well, you know..."

But we changed gears here, and I've tried to warn John [Block] about some of the things – I remember when Ezra Taft Benson was Secretary of Agriculture. And he was out in the country and hearing reports from people in the farm areas and talking to them, and at one place there was a fellow that was giving him a really bad time, really complaining. And Ezra turned around and looked at some notes that someone handed him and then turned back and said, "Well, now, wait a minute." He said, "You didn't have it so bad." He said, "You had 26 inches of rain this last year." And the fellow said, "Yes, I remember the night it happened."

***

03/17/81
National Association of State Departments of Agriculture: Remarks at a Dinner Honoring Secretary of Agriculture John R. Block

And I know once when I was out on the mashed potato circuit before I – well, that was when I was unemployed, between jobs – I was speaking to a farm group in Las Vegas. And on the way in to where I was to speak, there was one of those fellows that was there for the action, and he recognized me. And he said, "What are you doing here?" And I told him why. He said, "What are a bunch of farmers doing in Las Vegas?" And I just couldn't help it. I said, "Buster, they're in a business that makes a Las Vegas crap table look like a guaranteed annual income."

***

12/09/82
Dinner Honoring the Republican Majority in the Senate: Remarks at the Dinner

Now, I mentioned fishing, and that should remind me of a story. But the funny thing is the story it reminds me of has much more to do with the business we're in today than it does of fishing. It seems that in a small river town there was a young man named Elmer, who was so talented at fishing that he finally aroused the suspicions of the fish and game people because he came in with such a great catch every trip out. And the game warden asked the local sheriff, who was a very close friend of this young man, Elmer, if he would find out what was going on. So, the sheriff one day just casually suggested to Elmer that he join him on the fishing trip.

And they rowed out into the middle of the river together, and, once out there, Elmer took out a stick of dynamite, lighted the fuse, tossed it in the water, and after the explosion, the surface of the water was covered with fish, which he began to pick up. And the sheriff looked at him and said, "Elmer, do you realize that you have just committed a felony?" And Elmer reached in the tackle box, pulled out another stick of dynamite, lighted the fuse, handed it to the sheriff, and said, "Did you come here to talk or fish?"

***

HOLLYWOOD FRIENDS

12/04/83

Kennedy Center Honors: Remarks at a White House Reception for the Honorees

Now, the last two artists that we're honoring tonight are special friends of Nancy's and mine: Frank Sinatra and Jimmy Stewart.

Francis Albert Sinatra was born in Hoboken, New Jersey, and started to like music when his uncle gave him a ukulele. And one day in 1936, he went to a Jersey City vaudeville house to see Bing Crosby. After the show, Frank suddenly announced that he was becoming a singer.

In 1937 his group, the Hoboken Four, won first prize on Major Bowes' Original Amateur Hour. And for the next year and a half, he sang at the Rusty Cabin, a north Jersey roadhouse, for $15 a week. Let me repeat that. For a year and a half – Frank Sinatra worked for $15 a week. But it paid off. He got a $10-a-week raise.

*** ***

12/04/83

Kennedy Center Honors: Remarks at a White House Reception for the Honorees

We think of the Stewart character as open, kind, and honest – just like the boy next door. Well, Nancy and I and his friends can tell you that that's not just some screen character: that's the real Jimmy Stewart.

You know, there's a story I have to tell. When Jack Warner, head of Warner Brothers, first heard, that I was running for Governor of California, he said. "No, no, Jimmy Stewart for Governor. Reagan for best friend."

*** ***

OPTIMISM

09/05/84

"Choosing a Future" Conference: Remarks at the Conference in Chicago, Illinois

All my life, I've believed in miracles. I believe that if you truly have faith, your dream will come true. And now after 39 years of waiting, the miracle is happening. The Chicago Cubs are on their way to a National League pennant.

I have to tell you what that means to me personally. I was broadcasting the Cubs in 1935 when the only mathematical chance they had to win the pennant was to win the last 21 games of the season – and they did! And it still stands today as an unequalled record. When I'm in the presence of such greatness, how can I feel intimidated by a little challenge like running for President?

*** ***

01/20/82

Reagan Administration Executive Forum: Remarks to Presidential Appointees on the First Anniversary of the Inauguration

This is an exciting time to be alive, an exciting time to be in Washington, a time of both challenge and reaffirmation. Each of us has been put here for a purpose. We must redress past errors, errors that have already cost the people we serve far too much in economic stagnation, joblessness, crippling taxes, and inflation. It isn't going to be easy; nothing really worth achieving ever is. But this is an optimistic nation, and I am optimistic. If I wasn't I'd never have left the ranch to come here in the first place.

Now, you know there's a simple definition for an optimist and a pessimist. An optimist asks, "Will you please pass the cream? A pessimist says, "Is there any milk in that pitcher?"

But there's a story that maybe some of you know, and I just can't resist at this point telling it, because it has to do with the definition of optimism. A man who had two sons, and he was very disturbed about them. One was a pessimist beyond recall, and the other was an optimist beyond reason. He talked to a child psychiatrist who made a suggestion. He said, "I think we can fix that." He said, "We'll get a room and we'll fill it with the most wonderful toys any boy ever had." "And," he said, "we'll put the pessimist in and when he finds out they're for him, he'll get over being a pessimist."

His father said, "What will you do about the optimist?" "Well," he said, "I have a friend who's got a racing stable and they clean out the stalls every morning. And," he said, "I can get quite an amount of that substance. And," he said, "we'll put that in another room, and when the optimist who's seen his brother get all those toys is then shown into that room and that's there, he'll get over being an optimist."

Well, they did, and they waited about 5 minutes. And then they opened the door, and the pessimist was sitting there crying as if his heart would break. He said, "I know somebody's going to come in and take these away from me."

Then they went down to the other room and they opened the door and there was the kid happy as a clam, throwing that stuff over his shoulder as fast as he could. And they said, "What are you doing?" And he says, "There's got to be a pony in here somewhere."

*** * ***

HUMAN NATURE

10/04/88

Remarks at the Annual Dinner of the Republican Governors Club

How do you do? Thank you very much. Well, I want you all to know how delighted I am that you are here with us again. And you know, whenever I come to one of these fundraisers, I think of the couple that never once during the long years of childrearing took a vacation. But then in retirement, they wanted to take a trip to Florida, and they asked their sons for some money. And the first son was a lawyer, and he said, "No, I can't do it. I'm just fitting out a new law office and sending my son to an expensive camp." So, they asked their second son, a doctor. But he said, "No, I'm sorry. I can't. I've just bought a new house, and my wife is putting in a new kitchen." Then they asked the third son, who was an engineer. And he replied, "It just would be impossible for me to do it. I have just bought a big boat for the family and am remodeling our summer home on the lake." Finally the father pleaded, "Look, we've worked all our lives, not 1 day of vacation. We never had any money except what we saved for your education. In fact, do you realize that your mother and I were so busy working, trying to save money, that we never took the time out to get a marriage license?" "And, father," said all the three sons in unison, "do you realize what that makes us?" He said, "Yes, and cheap ones, too."

* * *

09/08/87
Remarks at a Meeting with Senior Presidential Appointees (Administration's Agenda)

There was a fellow that was on his way to a mountain resort, and a policeman stopped him and said, "Did you know you're driving without taillights?" And the driver hopped out of the car. He was so badly shaken that the officer took pity on him and said, "Well, now, wait a minute. Calm down. It's not that serious an infraction." The fellow said, "It may not mean much to you, but to me it means I've lost my trailer, a wife, and four kids!"

* * *

12/02/85
Remarks at a Fundraising Luncheon for Senator Slade Forton (Seattle, Washington)

There's a story – you knew I'd have story – about a fellow who had a different kind of job in mind, but he was out there working for the job. And then he saw an ad in the help wanted ads, where the zoo wanted a worker at the zoo, and he immediately applied because he had always wanted to work and loved to work with animals. And when he got there, though, he found that the job was to put on a gorilla suit, sit in the cage, and be the gorilla for the people who came to visit the zoo. Their old gorilla had died, and they had not yet received delivery of his successor. Well, he was a little upset by that, but then they explained that it would only be temporary and then he would have a legitimate job in the zoo. So, he took the job. And pretty soon he got a little bored just sitting there in that cage and people coming by, so he began doing tricks, particularly for the children that had come by to see the gorilla. And there was a rope in there and he'd get on the rope, and he'd swing around, and he was kind of getting into the act pretty good. And one day, very rambunctious, he swung so far on the rope that he landed in the lion's cage. And the lion started for him, and he stood up, and he started screaming, "Get me out of here. Get me out of here." And the lion jumped on him and said, "Shut up, or you'll get both of us fired."

* * *

07/15/87
Remarks at a White House Briefing (Minority Business Owners)

You know, I can confess to this group that I've been accused of being pro-business. Well, I just have to say: Guilty as charged. That doesn't mean, however, that I think business is always perfect and that things can't go wrong. Like the story of the businessman who called his partner up late at night, sounded very panicky, and he said, "There's $20,000 missing from the safe. What should I do?" His partner said, "Put it back."

* * *

05/14/86
Remarks to the Tax Reform Action (Tax Reform)

The special interests in the Nation's Capital here seem to have taken the taxpayers for granted once too often. It reminds me a little bit of a story, and I hope I haven't told you this story before. But if I have, you've got to remember that life not only begins at 40, but so does the tendency to start telling stories over and over again.

It's about a businessman who – just down at the entrance of his building there was an elderly lady selling pretzels. And every day he'd go by and he'd put a quarter down, and never take a pretzel, and go on in. He was being very charitable. And this went on for some time. And he came along one day, put down his quarter, started – and she took him by the arm. And he looked at her, and he said, "Well, you probably want to know why for this full year I've been leaving 25 cents on the plate and not taking a pretzel." And she said, "No, I just wanted to tell you that pretzels are 35 cents now."

* * *

THE PRESS

06/10/86

Remarks at a White House Briefing (Tax Reform)

What we do will determine what headlines are written about tax reform. Now, I know that some of you are no beginners when it comes to writing headlines. It reminds me a little bit of the cub reporter – you knew that something would remind me of a story – a cub reporter whose first solo assignment was interviewing a fellow who was just going to have a birthday that made him the oldest person in town. And he got to the address – it was an older building out on the outskirts of the city; an elderly gentleman ushered him in. And he sat down, and the reporter determined he was the man. And he said he was there for the interview, and he led right to the matter about how old are you, and the gentleman said, "96." He said, "To what do you attribute your longevity?" And the fellow said, "I don't smoke, drink, or run around with wild women." And at that moment there was a crash from upstairs. And the reporter looked up and he said, "What was that?" and the old boy said, "Oh, that's dad, he's drunk again."

* * *

04/13/88

Remarks at the Annual Convention of the American Society of Newspaper Editors

But as you may know, historians trace the Presidential press conference back to a Chief Executive who was quite reticent with the press, John Quincy Adams. He didn't hold press conferences. But it seems that every morning before dawn Adams would hike down to the Potomac, strip off his clothes, and swim. And one summer day, a woman of the press, under orders from her editor, followed him. And after he'd plunged into the water, she popped from the bushes, sat on his clothes, and demanded an interview. And she told him that if he tried to wade ashore, she'd scream. So, Adams held the first press conference up to his neck in water. I know how he felt.

But I've always believed that the key to good press relations is tact, candor, and seeing most things from the point of view of editors and reporters. Sort of like Lyndon Johnson. There's a story about Johnson when he was Vice President. He was coming off the Senate floor when he ran into a reporter for *The New York Times.* Johnson grabbed him, shouted, "You, I've been looking for you." Pulled him into his office, and began a long harangue about something or other. About halfway through, he scribbled a note on a scrap of paper, buzzed his secretary, and gave it to her. She was back in a minute with another note. He glanced at it while he talked and then threw it away. And eventually the reporter got out, but as he left the outer office, he saw the note that Johnson had written lying on the secretary's desk. It said, "Who's this guy I'm talking to anyway?"

* * *

03/14/85
Remarks and a Question-and-Answer Session at a Briefing for Members of the Association (Magazine Publishers Association)

And then, too, I think those of you in the press like a little candor now and then, especially if it's emanating from Washington. Seems that 25 of San Francisco's top bootleggers – this is a little story to illustrate what I've just said about candor – they were arrested back there in those days of the Volstead Act. And as they were being arraigned, the judged asked the usual question, of course, about their occupation. And the first 24 were all engaged in the same professional activity. Each claimed he was a realtor. And then he got to the last one, the 25th, and says, "And what are you?" he asked the last prisoner. And the fellow says, "Your Honor, I'm a bootlegger." And the judge was surprised, but he laughed and he said, "Well, how's business?" He said, "It'd be a lot better if there weren't so many realtors around."

* * *

04/17/86
Remarks at the Annual Dinner (White House Correspondents Dinner)

He said that I was supposed to get up here and make the press laugh. Well, there's nothing I like better than a challenge, like making people laugh just two days after April 15th.

I understand that ABC is having some budget problems. The news division has already laid off three hair stylists.

* * *

04/21/88
Remarks at the Annual Dinner of the White House Correspondents Association

Ladies and gentlemen, this is the last White House Correspondents Dinner that I'll be attending. We've had our disagreements over the years, but the time I've spent with you has been very educational. I used to think the fourth estate was one of Walter Annenberg's homes.

As my goodbye, I'm not going to stand up here and deliver one of those worn out sentimental homilies about the press and the Presidency. Neither of us would believe it.

* * *

SPACE

03/29/85
Remarks at the Luncheon (National Space Club Luncheon)

Nancy and I have watched space shuttles take off and land, as you all have, and we've spoken with the astronauts. I've learned that space has some interesting characteristics. For example, sound doesn't travel in space. I'm not really going to believe that until I see Sam Donaldson [of ABC News] up there.

* * *

03/29/85
Remarks at the Luncheon (National Space Club Luncheon)
Arthur C. Clark, distinguished author of science and fiction, says ideas often have three stages of reaction: First, "It's crazy and don't waste my time." Second, "It's possible, but it's not worth doing." And finally, "I've always said it was a good idea."

* * *

03/29/85
Remarks at the Luncheon (National Space Club Luncheon)
In Dr. Goddard's case, *The New York Times*, claiming rockets would never work in the vacuum of space ridiculed his effort. "He only seems to lack the knowledge ladled out daily in high schools," the *Times* editorialized.
I seem to remember when they were saying the same thing about Reaganomics.

* * *

03/29/85
Remarks at the Luncheon (National Space Club Luncheon)
Personally, I like space. The higher you go, the smaller the Federal Government looks.

* * *

03/29/85
Remarks at the Luncheon (National Space Club Luncheon)
One fascinating aspect of space travel is, as Einstein pointed out: The faster you travel, the less you age. And now you know my real motive for supporting space exploration.

* * *

AGE

04/17/86
Remarks at the Annual Dinner (White House Correspondents Dinner)
I don't know about you, but I've working long hours. I've really been burning the midday oil.
You know, I received an invitation that said, "Please come to Ellis Island July 4th for the hundredth birthday celebration of an American institution." Somebody goofed. My birthday isn't until February.
And it really won't be my hundredth, although I've really been around for a while. I can remember when a hot story broke and the reporters would run in yelling, "Stop the chisels!"

* * *

04/21/88

Remarks at the Annual Dinner of the White House Correspondents Association

Larry also said that preparing me for a press conference is like re-inventing the wheel. That's not true. I was around when the wheel was invented and it was easier.

* * *

03/07/85

Remarks at a White House Meeting (National Newspaper Association)

Well, that brings up the story about a cub reporter who went out to interview a 65-year-old man who'd just won the local marathon. And the fast-paced gentleman explained that vitality was a part of his family heritage. "After all," he boasted, "my father's 90 years old and he's still swimming a mile every day." He said, "and my grandfather, who is 110, just got married for the third time." And the young reporter asked why he would want to do that. And the runner said, "Who said he wanted to?"

* * *

10/16/85

Remarks at a Dinner Honoring the Senator Upon His Retirement (Senator Russell B. Long of Louisiana)

Ladies and gentlemen, one of the things I've been trying to figure out is why anyone as young as Russell Long would want to retire. Now, of course, that's only a cue for a story I want to tell you, because, you know, in my position anymore I have to be very careful of whether there is any ethnic note to any jokes that I tell, but I find that I can still tell jokes about people getting old. They know I'm not picking on anyone. So, this doesn't have any bearing on his being too young to retire.

But it is a story about an elderly couple who were getting ready for bed one night and she said, "Oh, I just am so hungry for ice cream, and there isn't any in the house." And he said, "I'll get some." "Oh," she said, "you're a dear." And she said, "Vanilla with chocolate sauce." He says, "Vanilla with chocolate sauce." She says, "Write it down. Now, you'll forget, dear." He says, "I won't forget." She said, "With some whipped cream on top." And he said, "Vanilla with chocolate sauce, whipped cream on top." And she said, "And a cherry." And he said, "And a cherry on top." Well, she said, "Please write it down. I know you'll forget." And he said, "I won't forget. Vanilla with chocolate sauce, whipped cream, and a cherry on top." And away he went. By the time he got back, she was already in bed. He handed her the paper bag. She opened it and there was a ham sandwich. And she said, "I told you to write it down. You forgot the mustard."

* * *

THE MILITARY

07/23/86

Remarks at a Fundraiser for Republican Gubernatorial Candidate William Clements (Dallas, Texas)

I'm sorry I can't stay longer, but we're on our way to Florida tonight. And that's where Ponce de Leon, you know, looked for the fountain of youth. And just in case he found it, I've got a thermos jug with me.

But it is wonderful to be in Texas and see how all of you revere your heritage. As a matter of fact, just last week in Washington we saw a tremendous example of this when the whole Texas congressional delegation met with Ted Kennedy. And they were talking on about Jim Bowie and Colonel Travis, Sam Houston, Davy Crockett, and the glories of the Alamo. And finally Senator Kennedy started to feel a little uneasy. You know, he's from Boston, and people from Boston – they have a little pride of their own. So, finally, Ted said, "Well, golly fellows, haven't any of you heard of Paul Revere?" And you would have been proud of your Senator Phil Gramm. He piped right up. He said, "Sure. Isn't that the guy who ran for help?"

* * *

05/22/85
Address at Commencement Exercises in Annapolis, MD (United States Naval Academy)
As Presidents since Washington have noted, the way to prevent war is to be prepared for it.

And as obvious as that is, it's not always appreciated. There's a story about John Paul Jones' chief gunners mate. It was during the gore and thunder of that most historic battle. He was loading and firing cannon and carrying the wounded to the medical officer, cutting away the tangled rigging. And apparently in the midst of that first fight, John Paul Jones went below momentarily and changed into a new uniform. And as he emerged on deck a voice rang out through the smoke and fire – it was the British captain asking, "Have you struck your colors?" And the gunners mate, sweat and blood dripping from his body, turned and saw Jones now in his fresh uniform reply: "I have not yet begun to fight." And the gunners mate said, "There's always somebody who didn't get the word."

* * *

01/30/86
Remarks at the Organization's 13th Annual Dinner (Conservative Political Action Conference)
It reminds me of a favorite little story of mine about a career naval officer who finally got his four stripes, became a captain, and then was given command of a giant battleship. And one night he was out steaming around the Atlantic when he was called from his quarters to the bridge and told about a signal light in the distance. And the captain told the signalman, "Signal them to bear to starboard." And back came the signal from ahead asking – or saying, "*You* bear to starboard." Well, as I say, the captain was very aware that he was commander of a battleship, the biggest thing afloat, the pride of the fleet; and he said, "Signal that light again to bear to starboard now." And once again, back came the answer, "Bear to starboard yourself." Well, the captain decided to give his unknown counterpart a lesson in seagoing humility; so he said, "Signal them again and tell them to bear to starboard. I am a battleship." And back came the signal, "Bear to starboard yourself. I'm a lighthouse."

* * *

REAGAN CRITICS

05/28/87

Remarks at the Association's Annual Congress of American Industry (National Association of Manufacturers)

Well, you know, when I hear all the charges that our critics shoot at us, it reminds me of a story. When you get to my age, everything reminds you of a story. This one is about a fellow who went into the Army. In boot camp, he spent hours on the firing range learning to shoot. When he was done with boot camp, they gave him one of those medals that says "Marksman" on it. He went home – very proud – on leave, and near the edge of town he saw somebody's homemade firing range – a wall, and on the wall lots of chalked bull's-eyes, in the middle of every bull's-eye, a bullet hole. Well, he wanted to see who could shoot like that, and finally he tracked down a 7-year-old boy. He asked the kid, "How'd you do that?" And the boy answered, "I take my gun, I line up my sights, and pull the trigger. Then I take my chalk, and I draw a circle around the hole"

* * *

11/16/87

Remarks at the Council's Annual Meeting (American Council of Life Insurance)

After 4 years of amnesia our critics, God bless them, have all of a sudden remembered the word "Reaganomics." When I hear them talk about stock prices I can't help thinking of the judge who was questioning a prospective juror. And the judge asked the juror if he had any opinion about the guilt or innocence of the defendant. And the juror said, "No, your honor." The judge asked, "Do you have any reservations in your conscious about the death penalty?" And the juror said, "No, sir. Not in this case."

* * *

11/29/88

Remarks at a Dinner Hosted by Republican Members of the Senate

And sooner or later the other party is going to have to take the hint and put themselves out of their misery.

But, no, it's kind of like the story they tell about the great French writer Alexandre Dumas. They say that he and another fellow had a terrible dispute that could only be settled by a duel. The two men were both such good marksmen that they agreed to draw straws and the loser would shoot himself. Well, Dumas drew the short straw, so he took his gun, went into a room, closed the door, and then a single short rang out. And the people rushed to look into the room. And there was Dumas standing there holding the gun in his hand. "Gentlemen," he said, "a remarkable thing has just happened. I missed."

* * *

01/30/86

Remarks at the Organization's 13th Annual Dinner (Conservative Political Action Conference)

The liberal conduct of foreign policy reminds me of a little football game that was played at Notre Dame back in 1946, when Notre Dame player Bob Livingston missed a tackle. And his teammate, all-American Johnny Lujack, screamed, "Livingston, you so-and-so you," and he went on and on. And then, Coach Frank Leahy said, "Another sacrilege like that, Jonathon Lujack, and you'll be disassociated from our fine Catholic university." Well, in the very next play, Livingston missed another tackle, and Coach Leahy turned to the bench and said, "Lads, Jonathon Lujack was right about Robert Livingston."

***

RELIGION – Part Two

02/22/87

Toast at a Dinner Honoring the Governors (National Governors' Association)

It's been a pleasure to have met with you this evening and to have had this opportunity to break bread and to get to know you. Pardon me, but the circumstances remind me a bit of the story of the Christians in ancient Rome who are thrown into the arena there. And moments later, why, the hungry lions were released and came charging out at them. And before they could quite get to them, one of the Christians stood up, stepped forward, and said something. And the lions suddenly just laid down and refused to attack the Christians. Well, the crowd at the Coliseum got mad. They yelled at the lions. They were throwing rocks at them and everything, but they couldn't get them to eat the Christians. Finally, Nero called the Christian leader to his side and said, "What is it that you told the lions?" He said, "I simply told them there would be speeches after the meal."

***

11/18/87

Remarks on the Observance of the Office's 25th Anniversary (Office of the United States Trade Representative)

I heard a story recently about two fellows who were always on the same team. They played baseball together all the way from the sandlot games, through high school and college and finally right into the major leagues. And then, tragically, one of them died. It was about a month after the funeral, and his buddy got a phone call – picked up the phone and heard his friend's voice. And he said, "Is that you?" And he said, "Yes, don't be afraid. I just want to tell you what heaven is like." "Well," he says, "okay, what's it like?" "Well," he says, "there's good news and bad news." He said, "The good news is there's baseball up here," and he said, "and I'm playing second base, just like always." "Well," he said, "what's the bad news?" "Well," he said, "You're slated to pitch this coming Tuesday."

***

09/06/85

Remarks at a White House Luncheon (Women State Republican Leaders)

I remember, as a boy, a preacher in our church one Sunday, in the dog days of summer, told us that because of the heat he was going to preach the shortest sermon that we had ever heard. And he said just seven words: "If you think it's hot now, wait."

***

03/09/88

Remarks at the Dedication Ceremony for the Knute Rockne Commemorative Stamp at the University of Notre Dame, Indiana

It's a pleasure to visit once again the home of the Fighting Irish. With St. Patrick's Day coming up and after seeing those film clips, it brings to mind another deathbed scene. You know, apparently the town rogue of one small Irish hamlet lay on his deathbed as the priest prepared for the atonement. "Do you renounce the devil?" "Do you renounce him and all his works?" the priest asked. And the rouge opened one eye and said, "Father, this is no time for making enemies."

***

11/19/87

Remarks to Local Business Leaders (United States Chamber of Commerce)

A few weeks ago was Halloween. You know, there's a story about a fellow who dressed as the devil for a costume party. And at the party he had a little too much to drink. Being tipsy, he got lost on his way home. But he spotted a small church, and the lights were on, and he decided to go in and see if he could get directions. Well, it was a stormy night, and just as he flung open the door of the church, a lightning bolt, and accompanied by thunder, flashed across the sky. The congregation turned around, and there he was dressed in the devil's costume. Pandemonium broke out. Parishioners ran from the church screaming. They jumped out the windows and raced out the back door. After only a minute or two, the church was completely empty except for one lone, little old lady with a cane who slowly walked up to this fellow who she thought was the devil himself, looked him right in the eye, and said, "I've been going to this church for 40 years, but I've really been on your side all the time."

***

10/06/86

Remarks at a White House Briefing (President's Commission on Executive Exchange)

I can't resist. I've worn out a story that expressed the – that expressed the importance of brevity in a speech. It was told to me by a minister, Bill Alexander – [he] used to do the invocation for the Republican National Conventions, and he heard me speak once. And after he'd heard me speak, he told me about his first experience as preacher, and I've always thought there was a connection.

He said that he had worked for weeks on that first sermon. He'd been invited to preach at a little country church out in Oklahoma. And he went there well-prepared and stood up in the pulpit for an evening service and looked out at one lone little fellow sitting out there among all the empty pews. So, he went down, and he said, "My friend, you seem to be the only member of the congregation that showed up, and I'm just a young preacher getting started. What do you think? Should I go through with it?" And the fellow says, "Well, I don't know about that sort of thing. I'm a little old cowpoke out here in Oklahoma. But I do know this: If I loaded up a truckload of hay, took it out in the prairie, and only one cow showed up, I'd feed her."

Well, Bill took that as a cue. And he said an hour and a half later he said amen. And he went down, and he said, "My friend, you seem to have stuck with me. I'm just a young preacher getting started. What do you think?" "Well," he says, "like I told you, I don't know about that sort of thing, but I do know this: If I loaded up a truckload of hay and took it out in the prairie and only one cow showed up, I sure as hell wouldn't give her the whole load."

***

ANIMAL TALES

04/19/88
Remarks at the Electronic Industries Association's Annual Government-Industry Dinner

I know that I am not an afterdinner speaker tonight. And I assure you that I will keep that in mind. I will, as Henry VIII said to each of his six wives, "I won't keep you long."

* * *

06/05/85
Remarks at a Fundraising Dinner for Senator Mack Mattingly (Atlanta, Georgia)

On our way here in Air Force One, I was looking down over your countryside out here because most of the way from Oklahoma I was looking down at clouds. And I could say that it reminded me of a story, but actually, I wanted to tell the story whether anything reminded me or not.

It was about a fellow that was driving down a country road, and all of a sudden he looked out and there beside him was a chicken – he was doing about 45 and the chicken was running alongside. So he stepped on the gas, he got it up to about 60, and the chicken caught up with him and was right beside him again, and then he thought as he was looking at him that the chicken had three legs. But before he could really make up his mind for sure, the chicken took off out in front of him at 60 miles an hour and turned down a lane into a barnyard. Well, he made a quick turn and went down into the barnyard, too, and there was a farmer standing there, and he asked him, he said, "Did a chicken come past you?" And he said, "Yeah." Well, he said, "Am I crazy or did the chicken have three legs?" He says, "Yep, it's mine." He says, "I breed three-legged chickens." And the fellow said, "For heaven sakes, why?" Well, he says, "I like the drumstick, Ma likes the drumstick, and now the kid likes the drumstick, and we just got tired of fighting for it." And the driver said, "Well, how does it taste?" He says, "I don't know. I've never been able to catch one."

* * *

02/20/87
Remarks at the Organization's Luncheon (Conservative Political Action Conference)

You know these last several weeks, I've felt a little bit like that farmer that was driving his horse and wagon to town for some grain and had a head-on collision with a truck. And later was the litigation involving claims for his injuries, some of them permanent. And he was on the stand and a lawyer said to him, "Isn't it true that while you were lying there at the scene of the accident someone came over to you and asked you how you were feeling, and you said you never felt better in your life?" And he said, "Yes, I remember that." Well, later he's on the stand and the witnesses were there – the lawyer for the other side is questioning – and he said, "When you gave that answer about how you felt, what were the circumstances?" "Well," he said, "I was lying there and a car came up and a deputy sheriff got out." He said, "My horse was screaming with pain – had broken two legs. The deputy took out his gun, put it in the horse's ear, and finished him off. And," he said, "my dog was whining with pain – had a broken back. And," he said, "he went over to him and put the gun in his ear. And then," he says, "he turned to me and says, `Now, how are you feeling?'"

* * *

WASHINGTON: GOTTA LOVE IT

03/22/88

Remarks to Republican Local Officials During a White House Briefing on Federalism and Aid to the Nicaraguan Democratic Resistance

As you may have noticed, Washington, DC, isn't like other cities. Harry Truman, a man famous for saying exactly what he meant in a very few words well chosen, once said of Washington, it's the kind of city that if you want a friend you should find a dog.

* * *

03/22/88

Remarks to Republican Local Officials During a White House Briefing on Federalism and Aid to the Nicaraguan Democratic Resistance

Anybody who has come up through elected politics as a Republican knows how important that solidarity is.

It's like a story our first Republican President, Abraham Lincoln, once told when he found out all but one of his Cabinet officers ranged against him on an important issue. His story was about a man who fell sound asleep during a revival meeting and didn't hear when the minister said, "All of you who are the side of the Lord, stand up." Of course, everyone stood up immediately, except for this one man, who was still asleep. But the preacher was only getting started and bellowed out, "All of you who are the side of the devil, stand up." Well, at that the man woke up and standing as straight as he could said, "I didn't exactly understand the question, Parson, but I'll stand by you to the end. It does seem we're in a hopeless minority."

* * *

10/09/87

Remarks at a Luncheon for Members of the Council (United States Information Agency Volunteer International Council)

I remember one of my first experiences with government was as an adjutant for an Arm Air Corps base in World War II. There was a warehouse filled with files, and the files containing documents and records and so forth – but which upon going at them you recognized that they were of no historical value. And they were totally useless, their time had passed them by. So, we started a message in the usual military style of sending a message, endorsing it up to the next in command, asking permission to destroy those papers so we could make us of the files for current documents. And then the next echelon – they endorsed it up and up and up, and finally to the top command. And then back down through the channel it came, and the answer was yes. We could destroy those papers providing we made copies of each and every one.

* * *

06/23/87

Remarks at the National Conference of the Federation (National Federation of Independent Business)

Speaking of regulations, for some businesses, regulations became so excessive that it seemed there were always inspectors around and government paperwork to fill out. It reminds me of a story. At my age, everything reminds you of a story. This one is about a man who started his own business. He did well, then bought a summer home in the country. And because he was good-natured, all of his relatives and his relatives' relatives took this as an invitation to visit all summer, every summer. One day the man was sitting with a young third niece-in-law, twice removed – who'd ignored hint after hint that she'd overstayed her welcome. Finally he sighed and said, "There's no chance, is there, that you'll ever come on another visit here again?" "Why," she said, "Uncle, why shouldn't I come back?" Well, he said, "Well, how can you come back if you never go away?"

* * *

03/22/88
Remarks to Republican Local Officials During a White House Briefing on Federalism and Aid to the Nicaraguan Democratic Resistance

It's like the story about a Congressman sitting in his office one day when a constituent comes by to tell him why he must vote for a certain piece of legislation. The Congressman sat back listened, and when he was done he said, "You're right. You know, you're absolutely right." The fellow left happy. A few minutes later, another constituent came by, and this one wanted him to vote against the bill. The Congressman listened to his reasons, sat back, and said, "You're right, You're absolutely right." Well, the second constituent left happy. The Congressman's wife had dropped by and was sitting outside the office when she heard these two conversations. When the second man left, she went in and said, "That first man wanted you to vote for the bill, and you said he was right. And the second one wanted you to vote against it, and you said he was right, too. You can't run your affairs that way." And the Congressman said, "You know, you're right. You're right. You're absolutely right."

* * *

04/17/86
Remarks at the Annual Dinner (White House Correspondents Dinner)

I've been criticized for going over the head of Congress. So, what's the fuss? A lot of things go over their heads.

* * *

04/21/88
Remarks at the Annual Dinner of the White House Correspondents Association

Of course, I still have lots of work here. There is that Panamanian business going on. One thing I can't figure: If the Congress wants to bring the Panamanian economy to its knees, why doesn't it just go down there and run it?

* * *

05/29/86
Remarks at the Association's Annual Congress of American Industry (National Association of Manufacturers)

This is truly tax reform that is profairness, profamily, progrowth, and prosimplification. Now, that last isn't mentioned very often by all those who oppose tax reform, but it's important to everyone who has to deal annually with the Internal Revenue Code. Let me give you an example. Here is the last sentence of Section 509(a) of the code: "For purposes of Paragraph 3, an organization described in Paragraph 2 shall be deemed to include an organization described in Section 501(c), (4), (5), or (6) which would be described in Paragraph 2 if it were an organization described in Section 501(c)(3)."

* * *

ECONOMISTS AND STATISTICIANS

02/11/88
Remarks at the Annual Conservative Political Action Conference Dinner
So, believe me, I welcome this approach by the opposition. And I promise you, every time they use it, I'll just tell the story of a friend of mine who was asked to a costume ball a short time ago. He slapped some egg on his face and went as a liberal economist.

* * *

04/09/87
Remarks to the Students and Faculty of Perdue University (West Lafayette, Indiana)
Now, of course, this economic expansion has plenty of economists puzzled. I can tell stories about economists, because my degree was in economics. You know economists; economists are the sort of people who see something work in practice and wonder if it would work in theory.

You know, forgive me, but there's another one I can't resist telling. It seems an economist, a chemist, and an engineer were stranded on a desert island. And between them they had only a single can of beans, but no can opener. The engineer suggested that he climb a palm tree to a precise height, then throw the beans at a precise distance, at a precise angle. "And when the can hits," he said, "it will split open." "No," said the chemist. "We'll leave the can in the sun until the heat causes the beans to expand so much the can will explode." "Nonsense," said the economist. "Using either method we'd lost too many beans. According to my plan, there will be no mess or fuss and not a single bean will be lost." Well, the engineer and the chemist said, "Well, we're certainly willing to consider it. What's your plan?" And the economist answered, "Well, first assume we have a can opener."

* * *

11/03/87
Remarks Announcing the Nomination of Ann D. McLaughlin (Secretary of Labor)
You know, the Labor Department collects many of our statistics, and since coming to Washington I've found that statistics can be a little slippery. In case you're wondering, that's my way of sliding into a story. It's about a lemon-squeezing contest at a State fair. The first man got up, and he was strong. He picked up the lemon and squeezed and squeezed and got out 80 percent of the juice. The crowd applauded, and he pulled open his jacket, and on his shirt it read "Bodybuilders Club." The next man got up, and he looked even stronger. He squeezed and squeezed, and he got out 90 percent of the juice. The crowd cheered, and he pulled open his jacket, and his shirt said "Police Athletic League." The final contestant got up. He was thin and scrawny and slouched and a little weak-looking. He picked up the lemon and began to squeeze, and out came 150 percent of the juice. He pulled open his jacket, and his shirt said "State Association of Statisticians."

* * *

10/09/87
Remarks at a Luncheon for Members of the Council (United States Information Agency Volunteer International Council)

In our economic summits, where we all meet around a table, seven trading partner nations, and so forth – sometime back when the summit was in England, which meant that Margaret Thatcher was presiding, one of the seven at the table got a little out of line, I thought, and attacked her about… she wasn't being properly democratic in conducting the meeting and so forth. And I'm not going to name which country's representative it was. I don't want to embarrass him, but he really sounded off. And when the meeting was over, I fell in step beside her, going down the corridor. And I said, "Margaret, he had no right to talk to you like that. He was really out of line." Brace yourself, fellas. She said, "Oh, women know when men are being childish."

* * *

REAGANISMS

01/10/89
Remarks at the Franklin D. Roosevelt Library 50th Anniversary Luncheon

If I may just tell a little story here that isn't about F.D.R. but may give you an idea about how far away the Presidency seemed to me at that time – not too long after the day I saw the President riding in the parade, I took a train out to California and ended up with a movie contract at Warner Brothers. I was known as "Dutch" Reagan then, my childhood nickname. The studio didn't like it, so they called a meeting to discuss what my name should be. And I began to realize how expendable what you might call my identity was in this new business I was in. So, as they were throwing names back and forth, I was just sitting there listening. They acted as if I couldn't hear. And finally, as they kept going on and trying out various names, looking up as if there were looking at a marquis, I timidly suggested one they hadn't thought of, my real name – Ronald Reagan. They started tossing it around the table. And I'll never forget the scene. The top man said it over and over to himself, "Ronald Reagan, Ronald Reagan." He paused for a long moment and then declared, "I like it." So, I became Ronald Reagan.

* * *

10/13/87
Remarks to the New Jersey Republican State Committee (Whippany, New Jersey)

It reminds me a bit of a story of an agent that I heard about once in my old career. You know, back in the days of vaudeville, somebody aspiring to a vaudeville engagement or a career in vaudeville would find themselves on a stage in an empty theater except for one lone, cynical agent who'd be sitting down there in the front rows. And he'd usually be smoking a cigar and telling them, well, okay, what do you do?

And this young fellow came out and stood there, and he says, "What do you do, kid?" And the kid stood there for just a couple of minutes, and then he just took off and flew up toward the balcony and then flew around the theater a couple of times and sailed back in and landed on the stage. The agent took the cigar out of his mouth and says, "What else do you do besides bird imitations?"

* * *

02/11/88
Remarks at the Annual Conservative Political Action Conference Dinner

We had an actor that was in Hollywood, and he was only there long enough to get enough money to go to Italy, because he aspired to an operatic career. And then after some time there, in Milan, Italy, where he was studying, he was invited to sing at La Scala, the very spiritual fountainhead of opera. They were doing "Pagliacci," and he sang the beautiful aria, "Vesti la giubba." And he received such thunderous and sustained applause from the balconies and the orchestra seats that he had to repeat the aria as an encore. And again, the same sustained, thunderous applause, and again he sang "Vesti la giubba." And this went on until finally he motioned for quiet, and he tried to tell them how full his heart was at that reception – his first time out. But he said, "I have sung `Vesti la giubba' nine times now. My voice is gone. I cannot do it again." And a voice from the balcony said, "You'll do it till you get it right."

* * *

04/15/85
Remarks at a Reception Honoring 20 years of Service (Milton Pitts)

I'm going to tell a story that Milt [Milton Pitts] knows and he likes it very much because it's about another barber, one in California – and it's really true; It's not just a joke – and in a place that, before Washington, I used to go get my hair cut.

And one day, there was one of the regular customers in there with his regular fellow, and told him to really, you know, do it up right because he and his wife were taking a trip to Europe. And the conversation that followed then: Question from the man who was doing the cutting, and he said, "Well, where are you going?" And he said, "Rome." "Oh?" He said, "Yeah. We're going to see all the monuments and all the historic things and the Colosseum and all of that."

"Nah," he says, "you won't like it. A lot of those things aren't around, or you can't fine them, and there's nobody to show them to you." He says, "What line are you flying?" He says, "We're not. We're taking a ship. We're sailing." "Oh," he says, "that's a big mistake." He says, "The food is lousy. It isn't like you think it's going to be at all. You're going to be sick and tired and bored to death before you get halfway there."

Well, he went on that way about everything. And finally, sitting in the chair, he said, "And we've got an arrangement already. We're going to have a meeting, an audience with the Pope."

"Oh," he says, "you think you're going to see the Pope." He says, "You'll probably be in a line – 20,000 people. If you get within two blocks of him, you'll be lucky." And finally, getting the haircut, he said, "Look, will you stop trying to spoil the trip. We've been looking forward to this for a long time. Now, just cut my hair and be quiet."

And it was finished, and he went on the trip. A few weeks later, he's back and in the chair. And the first question was, "Well, how was your trip?" He said, "Wonderful." He said, "The boat – it was wonderful. We almost hated to get to Rome; we had so much fun on the ship. And the food was great, like the best restaurants you could ever imagine." And he said, "We saw everything in Rome, all the history of Rome. It was really wonderful. We saw all those things, and we had an audience with the Pope. Twenty minutes he gave us." And he said, "When I bent down to kiss his ring, he said to me, `Where did you get the lousy haircut?'"

* * *

SPORTS

08/13/87
Remarks to Nebraska Civic Community Leaders (North Platte, Nebraska)
And it's great for this old horse cavalryman to be in a place with the smell of hay and horses.

Speaking of horses reminds me of a story. When you're my age, everything reminds you of a story. Seems that this fellow was a great racing fan and was planning to go to the races on the weekend. And then for 3 nights straight, he dreamed of the number five. So, when he got to the track, he took that program, and he went right to the fifth race and looked down to the fifth horse, and there it was, and the horse was named "5-by-5." So, he saved his bundle till that race, and he bet it all on that race. And sure enough, the horse came in fifth.

* * *

10/26/88
Remarks on Meeting the World Series Champion Los Angeles Dodgers)
This one's about a minister who walked by the lobby of a hotel one morning and noticed a ballplayer that he knew by sight. So, he said to the player, "One thing I've always wondered: Why must you fellows play ball on Sundays?" "Well, Reverend," the player said, "Sunday is our biggest day. We have the best crowds, make the most money and, after all, Sunday is your biggest day, too, isn't it?" Well, the minister nodded his understanding and then added, "But there's a little difference. I'm in the right field." And the player said, "So am I, and the sun's horrible out there, isn't it?"

* * *

04/29/85
Remarks at the Annual Meeting (Chamber of Commerce of the United States)
Now, I know that you're all too busy to get in the game of golf. But that was just a sneaky way of indicating that I got a little story about golf I'd like to tell you.

Seems there was a fellow who had a little trouble connecting with the ball. And on one tee, he happened to put the ball next to an anthill. And when he took his first swing, he missed the ball and hit the anthill – sent a few hundred of them into orbit. Then he took a second swing, and again he missed and hit the anthill. As he wound up for a third try, one ant said to the other: "You know, it's about time we got on the ball."

* * *

09/11/86
Remarks at a White House Briefing for Business Leaders (Public-Private Partnerships Conference)
This is the story about the two friends who are out hiking in the woods and suddenly saw coming toward them over the hill a grizzly bear. And one of them dropped to his knees, started peeling off his boots, reached in his pack and pulled out a pair of sneakers. And the other one says, "You don't think you can outrun that bear, do you?" And he says, "I don't have to outrun the bear, I just have to outrun you."

* * *

SOVIET UNION

03/14/86

Remarks at a White House Briefing for Private Sector Supporters (Aid to the *Contras*)

I have to tell you right here, I have been collecting stories that I can absolutely establish are told by the people behind the Iron Curtain, in the Communist bloc. And they're stories that reveal their kind of cynicism about the system under which they live. And one of the more recent ones that I heard was about the man walking along the street at night in Moscow. A Soviet soldier called to him to halt. He started to run; the soldier shot him. And another man said, "Why did you do that?" "Well," he said, "Curfew." "Well," he said, "it isn't curfew yet." He said, "I know. He's a friend of mine. I know where he lives. He couldn't have made it."

*** * ***

02/20/87

Remarks at the Organization's Luncheon (Conservative Political Action Conference)

The notion that government controls, central planning, and bureaucracy can provide cost-free prosperity has now come and gone the way of the hula-hoop, the Nehru jackets, and the all-asparagus diet. Throughout the world the failure of socialism is evident.

There's an underground joke that's told in the Soviet Union – for example, about a teacher who asked one of the young students, Ivan, what life is like in the United States. And dutifully Ivan said, "Half the people are unemployed and millions are hungry or starving." "Well, then," the teachers asks, "then what is the goal of the Soviet Union?" Ivan said, "To catch up with the United States."

*** * ***

04/29/87

Remarks at the Annual Dinner (Republican Senate/House Fundraising Dinner)

You know, if central planning worked, we'd be getting our grain from the Soviet Union and not the other way around.

We hear reports from that country, for example – I collect stories about that country – of a 10-year wait, seriously, to purchase an automobile, and the customer has to pay in advance. And there's this story about a worker who saves and saves, fills out all the paperwork, stands in all the lines, obtains all the necessary approvals. And finally, at the last window, the last stamp is affixed to the documents. He lays his cash down, and the bureaucrat counts out the money and tells him to come back in 10 years for his car. The little man turns and stops, and he says – looks back and said, "Well, morning or afternoon?" "Well," the fellow says, "it's 10 years from now. What's the difference – does it make?" He says, "Well, the plumber's coming in the morning."

*** * ***

11/04/87

Remarks at a White House Briefing for Members of the Business Community (Canada-United States Trade Agreement)

It's like the story of the New Hampshire farmer who had just been to a meeting down in the town hall of the local Communist Party. He comes back all excited and tells his friend about how wonderful communism is because, in that system, everyone shares everything they own.

"Does that mean, Fred," asks his friend, "that if you had two houses you'd give me one?" "That's right, John," he says, "I'd give you one." "And does that mean, Fred, that if you had two tractors you'd give me...." "That's right, John, if I had two tractors, yes, I'd give you one." "Does that mean, Fred, that if you had two hogs you'd give me one?" He says, "Now, that ain't fair, John. You know I got two hogs."

* * *

05/21/85
Remarks at the Annual Conference (Council of the Americas)

One of the most damaging lies of our era is the falsehood that people must give up freedom to enjoy economic progress, which makes me think of a story – everything makes me think of a story – about three dogs, an American dog and a Polish dog and a Russian dog. And they were all having a visit, and the American dog was telling them about how things were in this country. He said, "You know, you bark, and if you have to, you bark long enough, and then somebody comes along and gives you some meat." And the Polish dog said, "What's meat?" The Russian dog says, "What's bark?"

I have to interrupt right here and tell you that on one of my visits – I won't name him; I don't want to embarrass him – but one of the heads of state that I met with on this visit, he gave me one while I was on the way. He told me the story about the two fellows in the Soviet Union who were walking down the street, and the one of them says, "Have we really achieved full communism? Is this it? Is this now full communism?" And the other one said, "Oh, hell no, things are going to get a lot worse."

* * *

10/13/87
Remarks at a Luncheon Hosted by the State Chamber of Commerce (Somerset, New Jersey)

Well, these days when those same critics talk about the last 6 ½ years, they remind me of a joke among dissidents in the Soviet Union. This one begins with a question: What is a Soviet historian? And the answer: someone who can accurately predict the past.

* * *

03/14/86
Remarks at a White House Briefing for Private Sector Supporters (Aid to the *Contras*)

That does, I shouldn't, I know, but that does trigger another one of those stories I've picked up from over there. They came to General Secretary Gorbachev, and they told him there was a woman in the Kremlin and she wouldn't leave unless she could see him. So, he said, "Well, bring her in." And they brought her in. And he said, "Old mother, what is it?" She said, "I have a question." And he said, "All right." She said, "Was communism invented by a politician or a scientist?" "Well," he said, "a politician." She said, "That explains it. The scientist would have tried it on mice first."

* * *

11/16/87
Remarks at the Council's Annual Meeting (American Council of Life Insurance)

And I couldn't resist in the last meeting with the General Secretary to tell him one of those jokes.

It had to do with an American and a Russian arguing about their two countries. And the American in the story said, "I can walk into the Oval Office, I can pound the President's desk, and I can say, `Mr. President, I don't like the way you're running our country.'" And the Soviet citizen said, "I can do that." The American said, "You can?" He says, "Yes. I can go into the Kremlin to the General Secretary's office, I can pound his desk and say, `Mr. General Secretary, I don't like the way President Reagan's running his country'"

***

03/22/88
Remarks to Republican Local Officials During a White House Briefing on Federalism and Aid to the Nicaraguan Democratic Resistance

Well, I've spoken for long enough. I'm reminded of the quip that Henry Clay once made when one of his antagonists in the Senate, in the middle of a dull and lengthy speech, turned to him and said, "You, sir, speak for the present generation. I speak for posterity." Clay interrupted him and said, "Yes, and you seem resolved to keep on speaking till the arrival of your audience." Well, I won't do that today. I've said enough.

Thank you all very much. God bless you all. Thank you.

***

www.ingramcontent.com/pod-product-compliance
Lightning Source LLC
Chambersburg PA
CBHW051948280526
45789CB00009B/3219